MW00635658

The Essentials of Special Education Advocacy

Special Education Law, Policy, and Practice
Series Editors

Mitchell L. Yell, PhD, University of South Carolina
David F. Bateman, PhD, American Institutes for Research

The *Special Education Law, Policy, and Practice* series highlights current trends and legal issues in the education of students with disabilities. The books in this series link legal requirements with evidence-based instruction and highlight practical applications for working with students with disabilities. The titles in the *Special Education Law, Policy, and Practice* series are designed not only to be required textbooks for general education and special education preservice teacher education programs but are also designed for practicing teachers, education administrators, principals, school counselors, school psychologists, parents, and others interested in improving the lives of students with disabilities. The *Special Education Law, Policy, and Practice* series is committed to research-based practices working to provide appropriate and meaningful educational programming for students with disabilities and their families.

Titles in Series

The Essentials of Special Education Law by Andrew M. Markelz and David F. Bateman

Special Education Law Annual Review 2020 by David F. Bateman, Mitchell L. Yell, and Kevin P. Brady

Developing Educationally Meaningful and Legally Sound IEPs by Mitchell L. Yell, David F. Bateman, and James G. Shriner

Sexuality Education for Students with Disabilities by Thomas C. Gibbon, Elizabeth A. Harkins Monaco, and David F. Bateman

Creating Positive Elementary Classrooms: Preventing Behavior Challenges to Promote Learning by Stephen W. Smith and Mitchell L. Yell

Service Animals in Schools: Legal, Educational, Administrative, and Strategic Handling Aspects by Anne O. Papalia, Kathy B. Ewoldt, and David F. Bateman

Evidence-Based Practices for Supporting Individuals with Autism Spectrum Disorder edited by Laura C. Chezan, Katie Wolfe, and Erik Drasgow

Special Education Law Annual Review 2021 by David F. Bateman, Mitchell L. Yell, and Kevin P. Brady

Dispute Resolution Under the IDEA: Understanding, Avoiding, and Managing Special Education Disputes by David F. Bateman, Mitchell L. Yell, and Jonas Dorego

Advocating for the Common Good: People, Politics, Process, and Policy on Capitol Hill by Jane E. West

Related Services in Special Education: Working Together as a Team by Lisa Goran and David F. Bateman

The Essentials of Special Education Advocacy by Andrew M. Markelz, Sarah A. Nagro, Kevin Monnin, and David F. Bateman

The Essentials of Special Education Advocacy

Andrew M. Markelz
Ball State University

Sarah A. Nagro
George Mason University

Kevin Monnin
George Mason University

David F. Bateman, PhD
American Institutes for Research

ROWMAN & LITTLEFIELD
Lanham • Boulder • New York • London

Published by Rowman & Littlefield
An imprint of The Rowman & Littlefield Publishing Group, Inc.
4501 Forbes Boulevard, Suite 200, Lanham, Maryland 20706
www.rowman.com

86-90 Paul Street, London EC2A 4NE

Copyright © 2024 by The Rowman & Littlefield Publishing Group, Inc.

All rights reserved. No part of this book may be reproduced in any form or by
any electronic or mechanical means, including information storage and retrieval
systems, without written permission from the publisher, except by a reviewer who
may quote passages in a review.

British Library Cataloguing in Publication Information Available

Library of Congress Cataloging-in-Publication Data

Names: Markelz, Andrew M., 1980- author.
Title: The essentials of special education advocacy for teachers / Andrew M. Markelz,
    Ball State University, Sarah A. Nagro, George Mason University, Kevin Monnin,
    George Mason University, David F. Bateman, PhD, Shippensburg University.
Description: Lanham, Maryland : Rowman & Littlefield, [2024] | Series: Special
    education law, policy, and practice | Includes bibliographical references and index. |
    Summary: "The field of special education has been built by advocacy efforts of
    families, students, educators, and people with disabilities. This book provides
    educators with the tools they need to advocate successfully for themselves, their
    students, and their schools"—Provided by publisher.
Identifiers: LCCN 2023014825 (print) | LCCN 2023014826 (ebook) | ISBN
    9781538172469 (cloth : acid-free paper) | ISBN 9781538172476 (paperback : acid-
    free paper) | ISBN 9781538172483 (epub)
Subjects: LCSH: Special education—United States—Handbooks, manuals, etc. |
    Special education—Law and legislation—United States—Handbooks, manuals, etc. |
    Special education—Parent participation—United States. | Children with disabilities—
    Education—United States. | Learning disabled youth—Behavior modification—United
    States. | Special education teachers—Job stress—United States. | Special education
    teachers—In-service training—United States.
Classification: LCC LC3981 .M27 2024 (print) | LCC LC3981 (ebook) | DDC
    371.9—dc23/eng/20230510

LC record available at https://lccn.loc.gov/2023014825
LC ebook record available at https://lccn.loc.gov/2023014826

∞™ The paper used in this publication meets the minimum requirements of
American National Standard for Information Sciences—Permanence of Paper
for Printed Library Materials, ANSI/NISO Z39.48-1992.

Brief Contents

Contents

SECTION III: ADVOCACY IN PRACTICE

Preface

The field of special education was built by advocacy efforts of families, students, educators, politicians, and so many others determined to elevate the rights of children with disabilities. As you will soon read, educational opportunity for students with disabilities has improved tremendously in a relatively short period of time. From near total denial of public education to individualized instruction, related services, procedural safeguard protections, and much more, one cannot help admiring the inclusive progress that has occurred. Yet despite this success, special education teachers are experiencing enormous pressures in more challenging work environments with fewer resources than ever. Chronic teacher shortages, insufficient investments, and an eroding valuation of the profession have created a downward spiral that threatens educational outcomes of students with disabilities. In the face of these challenges, we recognize that special education teachers and administrators cannot become complacent. The field of special education has not reached its pinnacle; in fact, much work remains! We wrote *The Essentials of Special Education Advocacy* to continue the progress of those before us and propel the next generation of change agents.

The first section of this book covers the foundations of special education. In doing so, the three branches of the US government are explored. For effective advocacy, one must first understand what the rules of government are, how laws and policies are made, who is involved in making and enforcing them, and how one can effect change within established systems. Then, a historical exploration of special education advocacy is presented because the evolution of special education must be known to clearly see the present and informatively affect the future.

The second section of this book presents a framework that teachers and administrators can use to guide their advocacy efforts. The Five Rings of

Advocacy Framework allows complex issues to be organized through defined spheres of influence. Analyzing an issue through the perspective of each ring allows people to understand who they are advocating for and who they should be advocating to. Each chapter in this section examines a ring of influence by answering what that ring of influence is and why it is important, common opportunities to advocate for within that ring, and how to advocate from that ring.

The third section of this book is called "Advocacy in Practice." Within these chapters, we identify and discuss in detail a pertinent issue in special education. We then use a fictional vignette to present a problem that many special education teachers may encounter. Last, we demonstrate how our fictional characters organize a solution and implement their advocacy efforts across the five rings of advocacy. This practical section combines the theoretical concepts of the rings of advocacy with real-world application examples.

The Essentials of Special Education Advocacy was written for a broad audience of preservice teachers, practitioners, and administrators. Each chapter is presented in a structured format to answer essential questions about education advocacy and how teachers and administrators can use their rings of advocacy to influence pressing issues of the day. We hope this book serves as a useful tool for any stakeholder who realizes the promise of educational opportunity and desires to influence the field of special education for the betterment of students with disabilities.

Section I

FOUNDATIONS OF SPECIAL EDUCATION

Chapter One

The Government

Ever since people left nomadic life thousands of years ago and began living in communities with defined borders, they needed to establish rules to organize and protect group expectations. The system of rules and the people who make and administer those rules is known as a government. How a government is formed and what rules a government should administer have constantly changed over time. There are a variety of factors that influence the belief of what government should be such as geography and climate, social and cultural conditions, intellectual and philosophical influences, economic organization, and historical circumstances. It is understandable that no two governments are alike because each country's government reflects that country's unique environmental, historical, and political ideals. The United States of America is no different. The US government today is a direct result of historical contexts such as living under monarchy rule without any representation in the English government. From 1775 to 1783, the American colonies fought England in the Revolutionary War to separate from the King of England and establish their own form of government where individual freedom and the consent of the majority were paramount. Although philosophical debates continue to shape the US government's role and responsibilities, the foundation was established in 1787 with the signing of the US Constitution. In this chapter, we will discuss the US federal government and answer these essential questions:

1. What are the three branches of government?
2. How are laws created?
3. How do the three branches of government and sources of law interact?
4. Why is knowing about the US government important for advocacy?
5. Where can I find more information about the US government?

WHAT ARE THE THREE BRANCHES OF GOVERNMENT?

For many years the American colonies lived under English law and constant authoritarianism from the monarchy of England. After winning the Revolutionary War, the writers of the US Constitution sought to establish a government that prevented a singular controlling authority from harnessing too much power. To achieve that goal, the US Constitution divides the federal government into three branches with specific roles and responsibilities to delineate authority. In addition, the US Constitution establishes certain **checks and balances** between the branches of government to ensure that no branch consolidates too much power (see table 1.1).

Table 1.1. Checks and Balances

	Checks on the Executive Branch	*Checks on the Judicial Branch*
Legislative Branch	• Can override president's veto • Confirms executive appointments • Ratifies treaties • Can declare war • Appropriates money • Can impeach president	• Creates lower federal courts • Can impeach and remove judges • Proposes amendments to Constitution to overrule judicial decisions • Approves appointment of judges
Executive Branch	• Can propose laws • Can veto laws • Calls special sessions of Congress • Makes judicial and cabinet appointments • Negotiates foreign treaties	• Appoints federal judges • Can grant pardons to federal offenders
Judicial Branch	• Can declare executive actions and regulatory laws unconstitutional	• Can declare acts of Congress and statutory laws unconstitutional

Legislative Branch

According to Article I in the US Constitution, the legislative branch (otherwise known as Congress) is responsible for creating laws. Through **parliamentary procedures**, Congress drafts legislation, debates the legislation, then votes to approve or disapprove the legislation. The legislative branch was established to create laws and closely represent the will of the people of each state within the United States of America. To do so, Congress is composed of two bodies: the Senate and the House of Representatives. A piece of legislation must pass both the Senate and House of Representatives before it can become law.

Senate

There are two elected senators from each state, totaling 100 senators. A Senate term is for six years, and there is no limit on the number of terms a senator can serve. Senators are elected by and represent the **constituents** of their entire state; therefore, each senator must consider the political desires of all people within their state when they propose and vote on legislation. Senators do have the flexibility to take more politically controversial votes because a six-year term provides time between elections for them to explain and defend controversial votes. The Senate is considered the body within Congress that slowly and meticulously, sometimes obstructively, debates legislation.

House of Representatives

The House of Representatives is composed of 435 representatives from each state who represent a portion of their state, known as a congressional district. Congressional districts average nearly 750,000 people (Desilver, 2018). Therefore, more populated states have more representatives than less populated states. A representative's term is for two years with no limit on the number of terms. A quicker election cycle requires representatives to be much more responsive to their constituents' political wills. Furthermore, congressional districts tend to be more politically homogeneous, which creates representatives with stronger ideological positions, as opposed to senators, who attempt to represent a wider spectrum of political ideology. The House of Representatives is considered the body within Congress that is more responsive to the shifting political winds of its members' constituents, allowing it to rapidly propose legislation accordingly.

Executive Branch

Per Article II of the US Constitution, the executive branch is led by the President of the United States. Not only is the president the commander in chief of the military but is also responsible for enforcing and regulating laws passed by the legislative branch. The Cabinet, comprising advisors and department secretaries, oversees specific areas of the executive branch and assists the president and vice president in carrying out their agenda and enforcing the law. Table 1.2 is a list of departments within the president's Cabinet.

Each department is an extensive organization with a hierarchical structure of authority with thousands and sometimes millions of employees (e.g., the Department of Defense). Laws that are passed by Congress are often written with vague language and rarely describe how those affected by the new law should implement the law. Therefore, it is up to the executive branch to explain the implications of the new law and provide guidance on how to implement it. For example, when the Every Student Succeeds Act (ESSA) of 2015 was passed by Congress and signed into law by President Obama, it became the responsibility of the Department of Education to disseminate the information to state governments and school officials on how the new law changed requirements that were previously the law under the No Child Left Behind Act (NCLB) of 2001.

Sometimes federal laws are comprehensive, changes to previous policy are extensive, and a vast number of Americans are affected. Other times, laws might be more specific and only affect a small industry or particular group. Either way, the executive branch is responsible for ensuring that the laws passed by Congress are applied and followed.

Table 1.2. List of 15 Departments Within the US President's Cabinet

Department of Agriculture	Department of Commerce
Department of Defense	Department of Education
Department of Energy	Department of Health and Human Services
Department of Justice	Department of Housing and Urban Development
Department of Homeland Security	Department of Labor
Department of State	Department of the Interior
Department of the Treasury	Department of Transportation
Department of Veterans Affairs	

Judicial Branch

According to Article III of the US Constitution, the judicial branch is responsible for interpreting the meaning of laws, applying laws to individual cases, and deciding if laws violate the US Constitution. Vague language in legislation often creates confusion among those who are charged with implementing the law. The judicial branch acts as a referee to clarify the meaning of laws and settle disputes between **plaintiffs** and **defendants** of lawsuits. Since the US Constitution is the foundational source of law, no legislative branch law nor executive branch regulation can violate the Constitution. The federal judicial branch comprises nearly 100 US district courts, 13 US courts of appeals, and the Supreme Court.

Three tiers of authoritative hierarchy exist among courts, both at the state and federal government levels. The structure of this hierarchy is similar between states and the federal courts; therefore, we will focus on the federal courts. A **trial court** (i.e., US district court) is the level at which the fact-finding process takes place—except in special education matters, where a due process hearing officer is the fact finder. A judge and jury hear the facts of the dispute; then the jury provides a verdict based on the strength of the plaintiff's or defendant's case. US district courts have **jurisdiction** over states based on geographic distribution.

If a plaintiff or defendant loses a case at the trial court level, they have the right to appeal the court's decision to a **court of appeals** (i.e., US circuit court of appeals). Because the facts of a case have already been established at the trial court level, courts of appeals do not have juries. Rather, three judges read written briefs and hear oral arguments from lawyers about whether the lower court's ruling should be affirmed, reversed, or modified. Judges' decisions are based on whether principles of the law were applied correctly. Geographic jurisdiction of the 13 US courts of appeals is shown in Figure 1.1 and listed in Table 1.3.

The court of last resort and the highest court is called the US Supreme Court (remember, states have a similar structure of state-level trial courts, state-level appeals courts, and state-level supreme courts). The US Supreme Court currently has nine justices, but the number of justices has changed in the past. The US Supreme Court receives hundreds of requests but only hears a small number of cases, less than 1% of petitions filed (https://www.uscourts .gov/about-federal-courts/educational-resources/about-educational-outreach/ activity-resources/supreme-1). The Supreme Court agrees to hear cases concerning important questions about constitutional or federal law. Sometimes the Supreme Court hears cases to resolve issues that have split US circuit courts with contradictory rulings.

Figure 1.1.   Geographic boundaries of US Court of Appeals and US District Courts

From "Circuit map in agency palette," n.d., United States Courts (https://www.uscourts.gov/sites/default/files/u.s._federal_courts_circuit_map_1.pdf).

Table 1.3.   The US Circuit Courts of Appeals

1st	2nd	3rd	4th	5th	6th	7th	8th	9th	10th	11th	12th	13th
ME	CT	DE	MD	LA	KY	IL	AR	AK	CO	AL	DC	FED
MA	NY	NJ	SC	MS	OH	IN	IA	AZ	KS	GA		
NH	VT	PA	NC	TX	MI	WI	MN	CA	NM	FL		
RI			VA		TN		MO	HI	OK			
			WV				NE	ID	UT			
							ND	MT	WY			
							SD	NV				
								OR				
								WA				

Note. The 13th Circuit is called the Federal Circuit and hears appeals on specialized matters (e.g., patents, trade).

HOW ARE LAWS CREATED?

The US Constitution is known as the primary source of law. It is the founding document that (a) outlines fundamental rules in how the US federal system functions; (b) establishes boundaries for governmental action; and (c) designates authority, responsibilities, and separation of power among the three branches of government (Berring & Edinger, 2005). Some provisions of the US Constitution are specific; for example, to serve as President of the United States, a person must be a natural-born citizen of the United States and a minimum of 35 years old and have been a resident of the United States for at least 14 years. Other provisions are general and vague, such as Article I of Section 8, which authorizes the legislative branch to spend money to provide for the general welfare. The writers of the US Constitution knew that societies evolve and that the principles needed to be applicable for future generations; therefore, described within the US Constitution are provisions that allow the federal government to make new laws, execute those laws, and interpret their meaning.

Since the US Constitution is the primary source of law, it has supreme authority over newly created laws; thus, new laws cannot contradict the US Constitution. For instance, the legislative branch cannot pass a law that allows an individual to serve as President of the United States at age 32. The judicial branch (which is tasked with interpreting the **constitutionality** of laws) would definitively nullify that law because it is in direct violation of the US Constitution. Although this is a clear example of a law violating the US Constitution, many instances are not as obvious and lead to extensive debates among the three branches of government about the constitutionality of laws and actions. We will discuss this interaction between the three branches of government when answering the next essential question.

Remember that the federal government and individual state governments are similar in structure. All 50 states have their own state constitutions that describe the power and authority of the three state branches of government, such as the legislature, the governor's office, and the court system. State constitutions are more detailed than the US Constitution because these documents detail day-to-day operations of state governments. States can provide additional rights to individuals that are not found in the US Constitution; however, states cannot deny rights found in the US Constitution (Yell, 2019).

Statutory Law

When people hear the word "law" they most often think of statutory laws. Statutory laws are laws passed by the legislative branch of government

(Congress). There are variations to the process of a bill becoming a statutory law; however, the likely first step is that a representative or senator or a group of representatives or senators propose a bill. Usually, the bill is proposed within a committee that is tasked with specific areas of interest (e.g., Budget Committee, Foreign Affairs Committee, Homeland Security). There are numerous committees within the House of Representatives and the Senate. A bill can be proposed in either the House of Representatives or the Senate, and sometimes similar bills are proposed in both chambers of Congress at the same time. At the committee level, details of the bill are negotiated and refined. If the committee majority votes in favor of the bill, it then passes to the floor of the chamber in which the bill was proposed (i.e., House of Representatives or Senate). At this time, all members of the chamber can debate the bill and propose amendments. If the bill is passed by a majority vote (sometimes a super majority [60 votes] is needed to pass bills out of the Senate), the bill goes to the other chamber for a vote. An identical bill must pass both the House of Representatives and the Senate before its final step toward becoming a law. It is a considerable task, but if a bill passes the Senate and the House of Representatives, the final step in becoming a law is approval from the President of the United States with their signature. Only then is a statutory law official.

The US Constitution authorizes the legislative branch to create laws; however, once a law is official, enacting and enforcing the new law is the responsibility of the executive branch. The powers delegated to the executive branch to carry out the new law is called regulatory law.

Regulatory Law

Statutory laws passed by Congress are often expansive and lack details. To help fill in those details, Congress allows the appropriate executive branch agency to develop **regulations**. These regulations will assist those affected by the law to know how to implement and enforce. Depending on who is affected by the new law, one of the 15 departments within the executive branch Cabinet will serve as the entity responsible for providing specifics to the general content of the law (see table 1.2). For example, any law that is passed concerning education will become the responsibility of the Department of Education. Within the Department of Education are numerous agencies with areas of expertise. Employees within each agency are tasked with disseminating information about the new law to relevant **stakeholders**, providing guidance on how to implement the law and what happens for violating the law. All this information is called regulatory law, and regulatory law has the same force as statutory law.

What happens if statutory or regulatory laws apparently violate the US Constitution? What happens if the executive branch is not implementing the statutory law as written by the legislative branch? The US Constitution authorizes the judicial branch to interpret the meaning of laws, apply their constitutionality, and adjudicate disputes. The judicial branch establishes laws known as case law.

Case Law

Case law is established when judges publish legal opinions following a decision on a court case that involved the interpretation of statutes, regulations, or US constitutional matters. These rulings carry authority and establish **legal precedent**. The US court system is based on legal precedent, meaning once a legal principle has been established, it is applied to other cases with similar facts. The tiers of authority and jurisdiction courts have play an important role in legal precedent.

Courts have **controlling authority** over courts that fall under their jurisdiction. For example, the Seventh Circuit Court of Appeals has jurisdiction over every lower court in the states of Wisconsin, Illinois, and Indiana. When the Seventh Circuit Court makes a ruling, that ruling has controlling authority over all courts within those three states. Lower courts within the Seventh Circuit jurisdiction must adhere to the circuit court's legal interpretation and apply that interpretation in cases with similar facts. The Seventh Circuit Court, however, does not have controlling authority over the Ninth Circuit Court's jurisdiction. But courts not under the jurisdiction of other courts do have **persuasive authority**.

Let's say the Seventh Circuit Court heard a case about providing special education services to a student with autism and ruled in favor of the student. A year later, a case with similar facts involving a disagreement about the same law is argued in the Ninth Circuit Court. The Ninth Circuit Court does not have to follow the ruling of the Seventh Circuit Court but can read the published opinion of those judges and be persuaded by their legal rationale to rule similarly. The strength of a court's legal rationale and justification for interpreting a law can persuade other courts to adopt their rationale and justification.

The US Supreme Court is the highest court and has the ultimate controlling authority. When the US Supreme Court rules on a case, all 50 states must adhere to the ruling and apply the legal precedent in all similar cases. Since there are nine justices on the Supreme Court, a majority of five justices are needed to decide a case. In lower courts with only three judges, a majority of two is needed to decide a case. Typically, one judge is selected to write the opinion of the court, which states the ruling and the reasoning for arriving at that decision. If there are judges in the minority, a dissenting opinion is written, which states the reason for disagreeing with the majority. Dissenting opinions are important and carry persuasive authority. Dissenting opinions can appeal to higher courts or the legislative branch to correct perceived judicial errors.

HOW DO THE THREE BRANCHES OF GOVERNMENT AND SOURCES OF LAW INTERACT?

In total, the United States has four sources of law: (1) the primary source, the US Constitution; (2) statutory laws; (3) regulatory laws; and (4) case laws. With these four sources of law, rules to organize and protect Americans and their desired societal expectations are achieved. The process of governance, however, is not easy. The three branches of government and the four sources of law often interact in opposing ways. Through a system of checks and balances, each branch of government has a means to respond to the laws of another branch.

Although the US Constitution is the primary source of law, it can and has been amended over time. In fact, the US Constitution has been amended 27 times, with the last amendment passing in 1992. The process for amending the US Constitution is quite onerous. First, an amendment may be proposed by a two-thirds vote of both the House of Representatives and the Senate, or two-thirds of state governments may propose an amendment. Then, the amendment must be ratified by three-fourths of state legislatures for passage.

Because amending the US Constitution is such a rare event, most interactions between the sources of law occur at the statutory, regulatory, and case law levels. Figure 1.2 lists each branch of government and particular checks that branch has on the authority of the other two branches. We know the legislative branch has the authority to write and pass statutory laws. The executive branch (i.e., the President of the United States), however, must sign a statutory law in agreement to enact the law as written. If the executive branch disagrees with the law, the president can **veto** the law, thus stopping its enactment. The legislative branch then has the authority to override a presidential veto with a two-thirds majority vote in favor of the law in both the House of Representatives and the Senate. According to the Congressional Research Service (2014), out of 1,484 vetoes since 1789, only 7.1%, or 106, have been overridden by the legislative branch. Although it is rare for the legislative branch to override a presidential veto, this check on the executive branch's authority is constitutional.

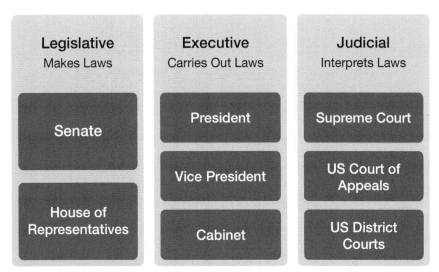

Figure 1.2. The Three Branches of Government

The judicial branch's check on authority is quite clear. Actions and laws by the executive and legislative branches can be declared unconstitutional and immediately halted. Interpreting the constitutionality of laws and actions, however, is quite complicated. Judges, just like everybody else, have a history of experiences that shape their personal beliefs, ideals, and actions. In general, interpreting the constitutionality of laws depends on whether a judge is an **originalist**, **living constitutionalist**, or somewhere in between these two legal text interpretation philosophies. In simplest terms, an originalist believes the constitutional text ought to be given the original public meaning that it would have had at the time that it became law (Calabresi, n.d.). Originalists argue that courts should be bound by the words of the Constitution, and the meaning of those words should be determined solely based on how they were understood when they were added to the Constitution. The critique of originalism is that the US Constitution is filled with ambiguous and subjective language that makes interpreting original intent challenging. For example, what does "general welfare of the United States" mean or what makes a search and seizure "unreasonable"?

On the other side of the legal text interpretation debate is living constitutionalism. Living constitutionalists contend that the US Constitution was intentionally written in broad and flexible terms to create a dynamic, "living" document that can evolve and adapt to new societal values and circumstances. Living constitutionalists would argue that the definition and legal application of "unreasonable search and seizures" should be done within current contexts with technological advancements to consider such as phone/internet tapping, satellite imagery, and financial banking/crypto complexities. The ability of the government to search and seize in 1787 was vastly different than in the 21st century, and living constitutionalists believe those differences should be considered when interpreting ambiguous language within the US Constitution.

If the judicial branch deems a statutory law unconstitutional, the legislative branch can either amend the US Constitution, which we previously discussed, or rewrite the law to be more in line with constitutional language. Other checks the legislative branch has is the ability to impeach and remove judges and the president. The legislative branch is also responsible for confirming the appointments of executive officials and judges, thereby, giving the legislative branch substantial authority in who serves in the other two branches. Taken all together, there are several checks and balances among the three branches of government and the four sources of law that are in constant fluctuation. The momentum behind the continual maneuvering between the three branches of government is rooted in advocacy.

WHY IS KNOWING ABOUT THE US GOVERNMENT IMPORTANT FOR ADVOCACY?

In the next chapter, we define and discuss advocacy, but it is important to remember that government is simply a system of rules by those who make the rules. To advocate for change, it is necessary to know who government officials are and how they make the rules. Regarding special education, substantial aspects are driven by decisions occurring through state and federal legislative, judicial, and executive branch processes (Kiarie, 2014). Understanding these processes and the four sources of law and how they interact will prove beneficial when discussing issues pertaining to special education. Knowing about the US government is needed to affect or change the rules for the betterment of your profession and the outcomes of students with disabilities.

WHERE CAN I FIND MORE INFORMATION ABOUT THE US GOVERNMENT?

Constitution Center

The Constitution Center is an interactive information source about the text, history, and meaning of the US Constitution. There is an interactive Constitution that provides the original text as well as various interpretations from a wide range of experts. The Constitution Center also provides a media library that deals with current issues around the Constitution. For access to these resources visit https://constitutioncenter.org/interactive-constitution.

USA.gov

An informative website that provides in-depth information about all parts of the US government. The website includes information about the three branches of government, including helpful infographics. For detailed information about the three branches of government visit https://www.usa.gov/branches-of-government.

YouTube

The video streaming platform offers a wide range of informative videos. Searching "School House Rock Government Videos" provides videos that break down the concepts of government in a way that makes them accessible to people of all ages. For a list of videos relating to the US government visit https://www.youtube.com/watch?v=tyeJ55o3El0&list=PLZxu8fzWW7cFh8z3UlDlWCERd6chwiqCu&index=2.

Harry S. Truman Library

The Harry S. Truman Library provides resources such as worksheets, crosswords, and games for support in learning about the branches of the US government. Additionally, it provides teacher resources and answer sheets. To access these resources, visit https://www.trumanlibrary.gov/education/three-branches.

KEY TERMS

checks and balances: US government system that ensures one branch of government does not become too powerful.

constituents: The people whom politicians represent from their electing district or state.

constitutionality: The condition of acting within accordance of the US Constitution.

controlling authority: Authority from higher courts over lower courts in their jurisdiction.

court of appeals: Tasked with determining whether or not the law was applied correctly in a lower trial court.

defendant: Person, company, or institution that is being accused of a legal violation.

jurisdiction: Authority granted within a defined field of responsibility.

legal precedent: A ruling that establishes legal principle and is applied to other cases with similar facts.

living constitutionalist: One who interprets the US Constitution as a dynamic document that evolves according to current societal contexts.

originalist: One who interprets the US Constitution as a fixed document where textual meaning should remain as intended when originally signed.

parliamentary procedures: Process by which the legislative branch drafts and votes on legislation.

persuasive authority: The written opinion of a court's legal rationale and justification for interpreting a law that another court is not obligated to follow but which may help inform the court's decision.

plaintiff: Person, company, or institution that initiates a lawsuit.

regulations: Instructions written by the executive branch that provide direction on how to implement and enforce laws passed by Congress.

stakeholder: An individual or a group that has an interest in any decision or activity of an organization.

trial court: A court of law where cases are first tried with a fact-finding process and a jury to provide a verdict based on the strength of the plaintiff's or defendant's case.

veto: A constitutional right of the executive branch to reject a bill or law proposed by the legislative branch.

DISCUSSION QUESTIONS

1. How do the legislative, executive, and judicial branches interact?
2. Do you believe judges should adhere to originalism or living constitutionalism when interpreting the US Constitution?
3. What do you know about other governments around the world? Examine other governments through historical circumstances, economic organization, and philosophical/religious influences.
4. What is the difference between controlling and persuasive authority?
5. Why is it important for teachers and school administrators to understand the structure and processes of the US government?

REFERENCES

Berring, R. C., & Edinger, A. E. (2005). *Finding the law* (12th ed.). Thomson/West.

Calabresi, S. G. (n.d.). *On originalism in constitutional interpretation.* National Constitution Center. https://constitutioncenter.org/interactive-constitution/white-papers/on-originalism-in-constitutional-interpretation

Congressional Research Service. (2014). *The presidential veto and congressional procedure.* https://www.archives.gov/files/legislative/resources/education/veto/veto-procedure.pdf

Desilver, D. (2018, May 31). U.S. population keeps growing, but House of Representatives is same size as in Taft era. https://www.pewresearch.org/fact-tank/2018/05/31/u-s-population-keeps-growing-but-house-of-representatives-is-same-size-as-in-taft-era/

Every Student Succeeds Act of 2015, Pub. L. No. 114-95 § 4104 (2015).

Kiarie, M. W. (2014). The role of policy in the development of special education. *International Journal of Progressive Education*, 10(3), 86–96.

No Child Left Behind, 20 U.S.C. § 16301 (2001).

Yell, M. L. (2019). *The law and special education* (5th ed.). Pearson Education.

Chapter Two

A History of Advocacy

What is advocacy? Although there are many definitions with subtle differences, all include components of active action and issue influence. In other words, advocacy is the activity of promoting the interests or cause of someone or a group of people. Given such a broad definition, anyone can advocate for anything. Throughout history, societal norms, expectations, and behaviors have changed due to advocacy efforts of individuals and groups promoting certain changes. In fact, special education was born because of advocacy (Fisher & Miller, 2021). Parents of children with disabilities, people with disabilities themselves, educators, politicians, and others saw a society that excluded children with disabilities from education. They disagreed with the societal norm at the time and acted to generate change. In chapter 2, we will discuss the history of advocacy in special education and answer these essential questions:

1. How has advocacy affected special education?
2. Who are some key historical advocates in special education?
3. Why advocate for special education today?
4. How do you advocate for special education?
5. Where can I find more information on the history of advocacy?

HOW HAS ADVOCACY AFFECTED SPECIAL EDUCATION?

When discussing the history of advocacy, it is important to distinguish between two terms that may seem synonymous—*activism* and *advocacy*. **Activism** is about making people listen (US Institute of Diplomacy and Human Rights, 2021). Activism draws attention to a particular issue through methods designed to grab attention such as protests, marches, strikes, or other means to make people listen—whether they want to or not. **Advocacy** is about identifying a problem, inviting all involved parties to listen to each other, and working on solutions (US Institute of Diplomacy and Human Rights, 2021). Throughout history, individuals and groups have relied on both activism and advocacy to promote change. Oftentimes, activists draw attention to a particular issue, followed by advocates who step in to create sustainable change and shifts in societal attitudes. Other times, advocates attempt to create change within the system but fall short of accomplishing their goals. A lack of progress can bring activists to the issue to grab attention and force people to acknowledge the problem.

Although both activism and advocacy are needed and have been used throughout history to bring about change, for the purpose of this book, we focus on those who employed advocacy for special education. We identify how and why advocacy can influence positive change within systems to alter attitudes, beliefs, and behaviors. Through advocacy efforts, sustainable change has occurred for students with disabilities in public education.

Before the Education for All Handicapped Children Act

Today, we know equitable treatment of people and inclusion of students with disabilities in public education are legally protected rights (Markelz & Bateman, 2022). But this was not always the case. Until recent history, people with disabilities were treated horribly out of misconceptions and ignorance. Although it is beyond the scope of this chapter to detail the extent that people with disabilities were excluded from society and their mistreatment in the centuries prior to the 1800s, the reality of disability history is the mass **disenfranchisement**, marginalization, and physical and cognitive oppression of people with disabilities (Martin & Rodriguez, 2022).

In the 1800s, schools for the deaf, blind, and physically impaired were established as the **stigmatization** of these disabilities decreased and advancements in educational pedagogy increased. What was deemed "normal" cognitive abilities of this population allowed professionals and politicians to suggest they had the intellect to benefit from education. Other people with neurological disabilities were simply classified as "feebleminded" or "idiots" and sent to institutions with often deplorable living conditions (Arnett et al., 2016). The ignorance of neurological disabilities remained entrenched in societal norms for decades and ultimately manifested in the **eugenics movement**.

In 1924, the Eugenics Sterilization Act was passed in Virginia, which allowed institutions and asylums the legal authority to **sterilize** inmates considered feebleminded, or imbeciles, without their consent. In a landmark Supreme Court case challenging the constitutional authority of the Eugenics Sterilization Act, a majority of justices upheld the act concluding that sterilization of the feebleminded was constitutional (*Buck v. Bell*, 1927). Supreme Court Justice Oliver Wendel Holmes described sterilization as a method appropriate to safeguard both the inmate and society, writing, "It is better for all the world, if instead of waiting to execute degenerate offspring for crime, or to let them starve from their imbecility, society can prevent those who are manifestly unfit from continuing their kind" (*Buck v. Bell*, 1927, para 4). It was not until Americans became aware that Nazi Germany was adopting US eugenics policies in the 1940s that the movement lost momentum (Black, 2012). Yet although sterilization lost popular support, the practice continued through the 1970s, and the *Buck v. Bell* ruling has not yet been overturned (Martin & Rodriguez, 2022).

Even with appalling policies such as eugenics taking place, the disability rights movement began developing alongside the civil rights movement in the 1950s and 1960s. A **catalyst** for change concerning the education of children with disabilities was the Supreme Court ruling of *Brown v. Board of Education* (1954, hereinafter *Brown*). The *Brown* case was about the constitutionality of segregated schools for Black children. Ultimately, the Supreme Court overturned the precedent (i.e., *Plessy v. Ferguson*, 1896) that established *separate but equal* and declared the segregation of Black children into separate public schools as a violation of the **14th Amendment to the US Constitution**.

Justices in the unanimous court ruling reasoned that education in society is of utmost importance. Negative consequences and stigmatizing effects of racial segregation harmed students of color and denied them equal educational opportunities. The court concluded that segregation based on an individual's unalterable characteristics was unconstitutional (Yell, 2019). Advocates for the inclusion of children with disabilities in public schools seized on the *Brown* ruling and highlighted similarities between the unalterable characteristic of race and disability. If segregating students by race was a denial of equal educational opportunity, then was not the exclusion of children with disabilities also a denial of equal educational opportunity? The movement for including children with disabilities in schools gained momentum after the *Brown* decision. Unfortunately, systemic change does not happen quickly. It was not until 16 years later that two seminal court cases examined the constitutionality of equal opportunity for children with disabilities.

In *Pennsylvania Associations for Retarded Children (PARC) v. Commonwealth of Pennsylvania* (1972) and *Mills v. Board of Education of the District of Columbia* (1972), the plaintiffs in both cases argued that states were disregarding their constitutional obligation to provide equal educational opportunities as supported by the equal protection clause of the 14th Amendment. The *PARC* case was about children with intellectual disabilities being excluded from public education (the term *retarded* was used at the time), but the *Mills* case was about all children with any type of disability. These cases brought critical concepts involving special education to the forefront:

1. Children with disabilities, regardless of severity, are capable of benefiting from educational programs.
2. Education is not solely defined as an academic experience. Functional life skills (e.g., communicating, feeding, clothing) are equally important and should be taught in schools when appropriate.
3. Since states had passed **compulsory education laws**, which required children to attend school and mandated free public education, states could not deny children with disabilities access to that education.

The *PARC* and *Mills* cases were decided in favor of the plaintiffs, and the exclusion of children with disabilities from public education was deemed unconstitutional. Because the *PARC* and *Mills* cases were litigated in federal district courts, the rulings only had **controlling authority** over schools in Pennsylvania and the District of Columbia. However, the **persuasive authority** of these decisions reverberated across the country. Within a couple of years, 46 additional lawsuits were filed in 28 states concerning the exclusion of children with disabilities (Zettel & Ballard, 1979). The outcomes of those lawsuits were similar, yet the adequacy of educating students with disabilities across the country varied greatly (Markelz & Bateman, 2022). Eventually, Congress realized the federal government needed to pass comprehensive legislation to protect the rights of students with disabilities. In 1975, the Education for All Handicapped Children Act was passed by Congress and signed by the president establishing the framework for special education as we know it today.

After the Education for All Handicapped Children Act

The Education for All Handicapped Children Act (EAHCA) of 1975—also known as P.L. 94-142—was passed to provide all children with disabilities between ages 3 and 21 access to a free appropriate public education. The EAHCA mandated many legal protections students with disabilities and their families have today. Six major provisions of the EAHCA were (a) nondiscriminatory evaluations; (b) parental involvement in the evaluation, placement, and service development process; (c) free appropriate public education

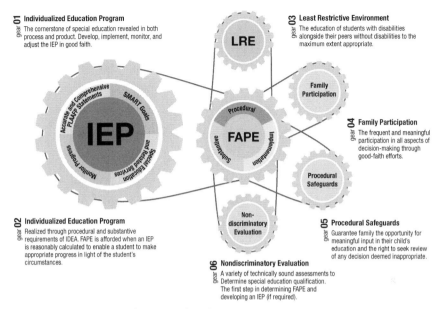

gear 01 Individualized Education Program
The cornerstone of special education revealed in both process and product. Develop, implement, monitor, and adjust the IEP in good faith.

gear 03 Least Restrictive Environment
The education of students with disabilities alongside their peers without disabilities to the maximum extent appropriate.

gear 04 Family Participation
The frequent and meaningful participation in all aspects of decision-making through good-faith efforts.

gear 02 Individualized Education Program
Realized through procedural and substantive requirements of IDEA. FAPE is afforded when an IEP is reasonably calculated to enable a student to make appropriate progress in light of the student's circumstances.

gear 05 Procedural Safeguards
Guarantee family the opportunity for meaningful input in their child's education and the right to seek review of any decision deemed inappropriate.

gear 06 Nondiscriminatory Evaluation
A variety of technically sound assessments to Determine special education qualification. The first step in determining FAPE and developing an IEP (if required).

Figure 2.1. The Gears of Special Education

(FAPE); (d) an individualized education program (IEP); (e) education in the least restrictive environment (LRE); and (f) procedural due process. Figure 2.1 represents and describes the six provisions (represented as gears) of the EAHCA and how each contributes to the central component of FAPE and how the IEP is the cornerstone of special education.

The enactment of the EAHCA was undoubtedly a major victory for students with disabilities. Yet once major legislation passes and implementation occurs, overlooked problems remain, and it is common for **reauthorizations** to take place over the years. For example, in 1986 the EAHCA was reauthorized to include services for children with disabilities between birth and age 3. In 1990, the EAHCA was reauthorized again to include transition services for students who were 16 years or older, and two additional disability categories were included: autism and traumatic brain injury. In addition, language within the legislation was updated to include "person first language," which also affected the name, becoming the Individuals with Disabilities Education Act (IDEA).

The judicial system also played a role in the evolution of special education after the EAHCA was passed. An immediate issue that arose was the definition of FAPE. Although the terms *free*, *public*, and *education* did not bring much confusion, the subjectivity of *appropriate* caused conflict between parents and schools. There is no distinct definition of *appropriate* because the meaning depends on circumstances. The individual strengths and needs of one student with a disability can vary greatly compared to the strengths and needs of another student. Therefore, the appropriateness of special education services depends on the individual child, and the interpretation of whether the provided special education services are appropriate can depend on the person (e.g., parent or school personnel). Referring to Figure 2.1, the IEP is the largest gear because the IEP is the primary evidence of an appropriate education (Bateman, 2017). The IEP documents a student's individual circumstances and the special education services provided to meet those circumstances. In instances that resulted in due process hearings, parents of children with disabilities were advocating for more services to meet their child's individual needs, while school personnel were claiming minimal services were sufficient to appropriately meet the needs of the student.

The US Supreme Court decided to consider the meaning of FAPE in 1982 to provide clarification and set a national standard. In *Board of Education of the Hendrick School District v. Rowley* (1982), the court developed the *Rowley* standard, which was a two-part test to determine if FAPE has been provided for a student with a disability. The two-part test asked the following:

1. Has the school complied with the procedures of EAHCA?
2. Is the IEP, developed through EAHCA's procedures, reasonably calculated to enable the student to receive educational benefits?

The first part of the test established **procedural rights** for students with disabilities and their families, for example, inviting all members of the IEP team to meetings, completing evaluations within required timelines, and ensuring families are aware of their due process rights. The second part of the test established **substantive rights,** which encompass the substance of a student's IEP and whether the IEP was reasonably calculated to enable the student to receive educational benefit. Examples of substantive components of an IEP include present levels of academic achievement and functional performance (**PLAAFP**) statements, annual goals and objectives, progress monitoring, related services, and others.

Although the Supreme Court attempted to clarify the definition of an appropriate education, the term *educational benefit* within the second part of the test created more questions than provided answers. How is educational benefit determined? Of course, parents wanted schools to provide the best special education services possible to achieve the highest levels of educational benefit. Many US Circuit Courts adopted a higher benefit standard that required IEPs to confer *meaningful* educational benefit. Other US Circuit Courts adopted a lower benefit standard that required educational benefit slightly more than trivial or *de minimis*.

Given a split among courts in interpretation of the educational benefit standard, in 2017 the US Supreme Court decided to hear a case called *Endrew F. v. Douglas County School District* (2017). The Supreme Court rejected the de minimis standard; however, it also did not adopt the higher standard. The ruling amended the second part of the *Rowley* two-part test to what is now considered the *Rowley/Endrew* test:

1. Has the school complied with the procedures of IDEA?
2. Is the IEP reasonably calculated to enable the student to make appropriate progress in light of the student's circumstances?

The definition of appropriate education can never be clear cut because of the individuality of each student; however, the Supreme Court ruling in *Endrew* reinforced the need for IEPs to be reasonably calculated through the incorporation of all provisions (i.e., gears) in **good faith**. Only then can the appropriateness and educational benefit of a student be determined.

WHO ARE SOME KEY HISTORICAL ADVOCATES IN SPECIAL EDUCATION?

The history of special education is filled with people and organizations that advocated for legal and educational protections for children with disabilities (Markelz & Bateman, 2022). One group at the top of that list are parents and family members of children with disabilities. Parents have advocated for their children to be included in public education through each branch of government (executive, legislative, judicial) at local, state, and federal levels.

Parents as Advocates

Mason Fitch Cogswell was a medical physician whose daughter (Alice) fell ill with scarlet fever and subsequently became deaf from the ailment. In the early 1800s, schools for the deaf did not exist; however, Dr. Cogswell was determined to figure out how best to educate his daughter. So in 1812, Dr. Cogswell contacted the General Association of the Congregational Clergymen of Connecticut to survey the state and find out how many other children were deaf (Martin & Rodriguez, 2022). In total, 84 children in the state of Connecticut were identified as deaf. Dr. Cogswell and these parents wanted an education for their children, and it was these parents who advocated for the first US school for the deaf.

A lot of work is required between identifying a problem and finding a solution. Dr. Cogswell partnered with a local clergyman, Reverend Thomas Gallaudet, who traveled to Europe to learn about educating children who were deaf (since no one in the United States had experience). Gallaudet found Laurent Clerc at the Royal Institute for the Deaf in Paris, and Laurent agreed to be Gallaudet's assistant. The two returned to the United States and cofounded the Connecticut Asylum for the Education and Instruction of Deaf and Dumb Persons. At the time, *dumb* referred to a person without speech. Today, the appropriate term is *nonverbal*.

Shortly after the school opened, it received a $5,000 grant from the Connecticut General Assembly, making it the first publicly funded school for people with disabilities (Martin & Rodriguez, 2022). Eventually the school changed its name to the American School for the Deaf. Overtime, the school's curriculum, based in manual communication, developed into American Sign Language. In 1864, Gallaudet's son helped start the Columbia Institution for the Deaf in Washington, DC, which is now called Gallaudet University. What started as one parent wanting an education for his child turned into a group of parents wanting the same thing for their children. This advocacy ultimately led to a new method of teaching, a new language, and a university for postsecondary learning! Although Dr. Cogswell and others pushed for change through the legislative branch (i.e., receiving a grant through the General Assembly to fund the American School for the Deaf), other parents have advocated for change through the judicial branch.

Timothy W. was born prematurely with numerous and severe developmental disabilities. When Timothy was 4 years old, the school board in Rochester, New Hampshire, convened a meeting to determine if he qualified for special education services under EAHCA. Timothy's pediatrician and other professionals reported that he was capable of responding to sounds and other stimuli and therefore should be provided with an IEP that included physical and occupational therapy. Other pediatricians and professionals in the meeting, however, reported that Timothy had no educational potential. The school officials determined that Timothy was not "educationally handicapped" because the severity and complexity of his disabilities prevented him from being "capable of benefiting" from special education (*Timothy W. v. Rochester, N.H. School District* [1989]). Timothy was denied special education services.

Timothy's parents refused to accept the school officials' decision and filed a due process complaint to the state of New Hampshire. Eventually, the case made its way to the First Circuit Court of Appeals, where the judges ruled in favor of Timothy and his parents. The court affirmed what is known as the **zero reject** principle of IDEA. The principle states that no child, regardless of disability severity, can be denied special education services. In addition, the Timothy decision also defined education in a broader sense to include nonacademic and functional skills, which are foundational for basic life skills (Brady et al., 2020).

Educators as Advocates

While parents were advocating for special education outside school walls, many educators were advocating for the rights of students with disabilities within school walls. One notable educator advocate was Elizabeth Farrell. In the early 1900s, Farrell was teaching at a public school in New York City. At that time, singular intelligence (IQ) testing was used to determine a student's abilities. A low IQ score meant a student had low potential. Farrell advocated for a variety of assessments to determine a student's strengths and interests to then develop an individualized curriculum. Farrell developed the concept of **specially designed instruction** (SDI), which is the foundation of how special education instruction operates today. Farrell also believed that students with disabilities could be educated in an "ungraded class" with the expectation that students could be reintroduced into the general education classroom (Kode, 2017).

Farrell's advocacy for teaching students with disabilities in ungraded classrooms gained momentum. In 1906, she was appointed as director of her special education program, officially called the Inspector of Ungraded Class Department. By 1911, there were more than 130 special education (i.e., ungraded) classrooms in New York City. Farrell's advocacy did not stop in New York City. In 1922, she was the founder and first president of the International Council for the Education of Exceptional Children.

Known today as the Council for Exceptional Children (CEC), CEC is the largest international professional organization dedicated to improving the success of children and youth with disabilities and/or gifts and talents. CEC advocates for appropriate governmental policies, sets professional standards, provides professional development, and helps professionals obtain conditions and resources necessary for effective professional practice (CEC, 2022). CEC has two goals:

1. Educators will be highly competent professionals entrusted to provide quality instruction that will enable all students to pursue their full potential.
2. CEC will have the capacity and capabilities to lead the field of special education in advocacy, standards, and professional learning and practice.

CEC was instrumental in assisting the passage of EAHCA (1975) and continues to advocate on behalf of its thousands of educator members to advance the success of children with disabilities.

WHY ADVOCATE FOR SPECIAL EDUCATION TODAY?

The previous section provided a brief history on the role of advocacy in special education. However, it is clear that public education would not provide the opportunities and services today for students with disabilities without the persistent efforts of many advocates. Parents, politicians, professional organizations, and many others must continue to advocate for special education. As educators, we, too, must maintain advocacy for our profession.

For Students

The education of students with disabilities has certainly improved over time from nonexistent to what it is today, yet more work remains to be done. Disparities in achievement, **disproportional representation**, and funding shortfalls continue to impede the success of students with disabilities. Specific challenges will be covered in subsequent chapters; however, the educational rights of students with disabilities have been and should continue to be at the center of educators' advocacy efforts. When Congress passed legislation to permanently alter the narrative about special education, they wrote that the purpose of IDEA was to do the following:

> Ensure that all children with disabilities have available to them a free appropriate public education what emphasizes special education and related services designed to meet their unique needs and prepare them for further education, employment, and independent living; to ensure that the rights of children with disabilities and parents of such children are protected; to assist states, localities, educational service agencies, and Federal agencies to provide for the education of all children with disabilities. (IDEA, 2004)

It would be naïve to think that special education has reached its pinnacle of progression and that current circumstances are the best we can do for all children with disabilities. As knowledgeable and experienced professionals, we must continue to identify problems within the system, invite key stakeholders to the conversation, and promote solutions.

For Teachers

Although students with disabilities remain a central focus of advocacy efforts, special education as a profession must also be prioritized, professionalized, and respected. The positive effects of a highly qualified teacher on student outcomes are well documented (Brownell et al., 2010). As teachers, we need to ensure that policies are made that elevate the profession with high standards so that students with disabilities are receiving the quality of special education services they need and are legally entitled to. Special education teachers are responsible for the design, delivery, and adjustment of a student's IEP. Special education teachers are critical in the actualization of whether special education is implemented as intended and effective as possible.

The responsibilities of special education teachers are vast and complex. Persistent progression of special education cannot happen without a strong special education teaching workforce. Realizing this necessity, the Office of Special Education Programs at the US Department of Education has launched an initiative to attract, prepare, and retain effective personnel (Ideas That Work, 2022). As we will discuss in chapters 8, 9, and 10, teachers are integral to solving persistent challenges in special education. Advocating for special education teachers must be prioritized.

HOW DO YOU ADVOCATE FOR SPECIAL EDUCATION?

In the next section and subsequent chapters, we discuss how special education teachers can advocate for special education. We contend that one should approach advocacy through a framework that identifies five areas of influence. We call these the five rings of advocacy (figure 2.2). Remember that advocacy includes the following:

1. Identifying and understanding the problem.
2. Inviting all stakeholders involved to listen to each other.
3. Determining potential solutions to enact change.

Figure 2.2. The Five Rings of Advocacy

By examining an issue in special education through the perspective of each ring, it allows one to understand *for* whom they should be advocating and *to* whom they should be advocating.

The first ring of influence is self-advocacy. It is imperative that special education teachers advocate for themselves as individuals and as part of a profession. Chapter 3 includes parameters for when self-advocacy is needed and helpful. Special education teachers need time, resources, and support to do their job well. Depending on the need, special education teachers may be advocating to other education professionals, building leaders, or families to provide appropriate special education services and positively affect their ability to do their job well and successfully affect the outcomes of their students.

The second ring of influence is classroom advocacy. Improving the learning environment for all students within a classroom or on one's caseload is the guiding principle behind classroom advocacy. Chapter 4 includes parameters for when classroom advocacy is needed and helpful. Depending on the need, special education teachers may be advocating to other education professionals, building leaders, or families to improve the educational experience of all students in their classroom or on their caseload.

The third ring of influence is school advocacy. School advocacy is where one seeks to find solutions at the school level rather than at the individual classroom level such as a change to school policies or procedures. Chapter 5 includes parameters for when school advocacy is needed and helpful. Special education teachers may recognize unique needs of students with disabilities that could be solved more universally than individually and therefore advocate to school board members or to building or district-level leaders.

The fourth ring of influence is state advocacy. State advocacy relates to leading change in state-level education policy and implementation guidelines that affect students with disabilities and the special education profession either intentionally or unintentionally. Chapter 6 includes parameters for when state advocacy is needed and helpful. Special education teachers, who have firsthand knowledge of the consequences, both positive and negative, of state policies after implementation, are well positioned to both recognize problems and understand realistic solutions. Through state advocacy, special education teachers advocate to their state-level elected representatives and department of education personnel.

The fifth ring of influence is federal advocacy. Similar to state advocacy, federal advocacy is also about leading change in education policy and implementation guidelines that affect students with disabilities and the special education profession either intentionally or unintentionally based on federal statutes. Special education teachers do not need to be policy experts to recognize the influence federal-level policies have on their ability to provide a quality educational experience for their students. Chapter 7 includes parameters for when federal advocacy is needed and helpful. Through federal advocacy, special education teachers can advocate as a member of a special interest group, organization, consortium, or coalition with other members who share similar concerns and have identified similar solutions or as an individual voting citizen by reaching out to federal-level elected representatives and department of education personnel.

As we will discuss, problems and potential solutions are not relevant to every ring of influence. Advocating for more planning time with general education co-teachers will likely consist of problem, solution, and communication within the self and classroom advocacy rings. More universal issues, such as chronic teacher shortages, may involve school, state, and federal advocacy rings. But most issues have potential solutions that leverage multiple rings of influence, and it is advantageous to approach advocacy efforts with an understanding of how each ring can lead to change. Therefore, chapters 3 through 7 will focus on the rings of advocacy and detail what each rings represents, why you should advocate for that ring, and how to advocate from within that ring. Then, in chapters 8, 9, and 10 we will demonstrate these concepts by examining specific scenarios that address pressing current issues in special education.

WHERE CAN I FIND MORE INFORMATION ON THE HISTORY OF ADVOCACY?

Essentials of Special Education Law

Markelz and Bateman (2022) discuss in accessible detail the six gears (i.e., principles of IDEA). This supplemental textbook distills the legal complexities of special education into a practical resource for preparation programs as well as professionals in the field.

Council for Exceptional Children

The largest international professional organization dedicated to improving the success of children and youth with disabilities and/or gifts and talents. Resources are available for nonmembers; however, membership provides substantial access to professional development opportunities. Visit https://exceptionalchildren.org/

US Department of Education

 The US Department of Education presents a *History of the Individuals with Disabilities Education Act*. On this web page is presented an outline with brief descriptions discussing conditions before the passage of EAHCA (1975) and relevant reauthorizations since then. Visit https://sites.ed.gov/idea/IDEA-History

Elizabeth Farrell and the History of Special Education

 Kode (2017) presents the inspirational story of a genuine American hero: the woman who "created" special education and devoted her life to making a difference in the lives of children with disabilities. This second edition book includes new original photographs from education archives, along with a new preface and epilogue setting Miss Farrell's life and work in context for teachers in the 21st century.

KEY TERMS

14th Amendment to the US Constitution: "All persons born or naturalized in the United States and subject to the jurisdiction thereof, are citizens of the United States and of the State wherein they reside. No State shall make or enforce any law which shall abridge the privileges or immunities of citizens of the United States; nor shall any State deprive any person of life, liberty, or property, without due process of law; nor deny to any person within its jurisdiction the equal protection of the laws."

activism: Using methods to draw attention to a particular issue such as protests, marches, and strikes.

advocacy: Identifying a problem, inviting key stakeholders, and working on a solution.

catalyst: A person or thing that causes an event.

compulsory education laws: Require children to attend public or state-accredited private school for a certain period of time.

controlling authority: Authority from higher courts over lower courts in their jurisdiction.

disenfranchisement: Being deprived of a right or a privilege.

disproportional representation: The percentage of students in special education from certain demographic groups differs significantly from their percentage in the general school population.

eugenics movement: The use of methods such as involuntary sterilization, segregation, and social exclusion to rid society of individuals deemed to be unfit.

good faith: With sincere and honest effort.

PLAAFP: Present levels of academic achievement and functional performance statements summarize a student's current levels of functioning and serve as the foundation from which all other components of the IEP are built.

persuasive authority: Written opinions by lower courts or courts of other jurisdictions that a court is not obligated to follow but which may help inform the court's decision.

procedural rights: Procedures that must be followed to ensure special education rights, as outlined by the Individuals with Disabilities Education Act (IDEA), are provided.

reauthorizations: The renewal of a law by Congress (sometimes with amendments to the original law).

specially designed instruction: Instruction that is tailored to a particular student. It addresses their individualized education program (IEP) goals, accounts for their disability, provides modifications or adaptations to content, and encourages access to the general education curriculum.

sterilize: Deprive a person of the ability to produce children, typically by removing or blocking the sex organs.

stigmatization: The disapproval or discrimination against someone or something.

substantive rights: Protections of the content and quality of educational services.

zero reject: The principle that no student with a disability can be denied a free appropriate public education.

DISCUSSION QUESTIONS

1. How has advocacy played a role in the progression of special education?
2. What are some other key advocates in special education?
3. Has the stigmatization of people with disabilities disappeared? Why or why not?
4. What are some issues in special education that require advocacy efforts?
5. What does the future of special education look like?

REFERENCES

Arnett, S., Fitzpatrick, M., & Theoharis, N. R. (2016). *Foundation of special education: Understanding students with exceptionalities.* Kendall Hunt Publishing.

Bateman, B. D. (2017). Individualized education programs. In J. M. Kauffman and D. P. Hallahan (Eds.), *Handbook of special education* (2nd ed., pp. 91–124). Taylor & Francis/Routledge.

Black, E. (2012). *War against the weak: Eugenics and America's campaign to create a master race.* Dialog Press.

Board of Education of the Hendrick Hudson School District v. Rowley, 485 U.S. 176 (1982).

Brady, K. P., Russo, C. J., Dieterich, C. A., & Osborne, A. G., Jr. (2020). *Legal issues in special education: Principles, policies, and practices.* Routledge.

Brown v. Board of Education, 347 U.S. 483 (1954).

Brownell, M. T., Sindelar, P. T., Kiely, M. T., & Danielson, L. C. (2010). Special education teacher quality and preparation: Exposing foundations, constructing a new model. *Exceptional Children, 76*(3), 357–377.

Buck v. Bell, 274 U.S. 200 (1927).

Council for Exceptional Children. (2022). *About us.* https://exceptionalchildren.org/about-us

Education for All Handicapped Children Act of 1975, 20 U.S.C. § 1401.

Endrew F. v. Douglas County School District, 137 S. Ct. 988 (2017).

Fisher, K., & Miller, K. M. (2021). Legislative advocacy for special educators. *TEACHING Exceptional Children, 53*(3), 244–252.

Ideas That Work. (2022). *Attract, prepare, retain: Effective personnel for all.* https://osepideasthatwork.org/attract-prepare-retain-effective-personnel-all

Individuals with Disabilities Education Act of 2004, 20 U.S.C. § 1400.

Kode, K. (2017). *Elizabeth Farrell and the history of special education* (2nd ed.). Council for Exceptional Children.

Markelz, A. M., & Bateman, D. F. (2022). *The essentials of special education law.* Rowman & Littlefield.

Martin, E., & Rodriquez, J. A. (2022). Historical foundations of special education law: A civil rights movement. In W. Murkowski & J. Rodriguez (Eds.), *Special education law and policy: From foundation to application.* Plural Publishing.

Mills v. Board of Education of the District of Columbia, 358 F. Supp. 866 (D.D.C. 1972).

Pennsylvania Association for Retarded Children (PARC) v. Commonwealth of Pennsylvania, 343 F. Supp. 279 (E.D. Pa. 1972).

Plessy v. Ferguson, 163 U.S. 537 (1896).

Timothy W. v. Rochester, N.H. School District, 875 F.2d 954 (1st Cir. 1989).

US Institute of Diplomacy and Human Rights. (2021). *Activism versus advocacy: What is human rights advocacy?* https://usidhr.org/activism-vs-advocacy/

Yell, M. L. (2019). *The law and special education* (5th ed.). Pearson Education.

Zettel, J. J., & Ballard, J. (1979). The Education for All Handicapped Children Act of 1975 PL 94-142: Its history, origins, and concepts. *Journal of Education, 161*(3), 5–22.

RINGS OF ADVOCACY

Chapter Three

Ring of Self-Advocacy

The history of special education is filled with individuals who advocated for access to educational opportunities and civil rights equality. Although improving the outcomes of students is always at the forefront of an educator's mind, it is equally important that educators have job satisfaction and positively view their professional growth. It is no surprise, then, that student outcomes and job satisfaction are intricately linked. Yet teachers face many barriers that influence their ability to do their job well and affect the outcomes of their students. In this chapter, we discuss self-advocacy as a primary point of influence every special education teacher or administrator should advocate for (figure 3.1). The self-advocacy ring of influence is critical in maintaining

Figure 3.1. Self-Advocacy Ring

the progress of special education. Just as so many have advocated in the past, you, too, must continue to propel the profession toward a more just, equitable, and respected future. In chapter 3, we will answer these essential questions:

1. What is the self-advocacy ring and why is it important?
2. What are some current opportunities for self-advocacy?
3. How do you advocate for yourself?
4. Where can I find more information on self-advocacy?

WHAT IS THE SELF-ADVOCACY RING AND WHY IS IT IMPORTANT?

If advocacy is the activity of promoting the interest or cause of someone, then self-advocacy is the activity of promoting one's own interests. Self-advocacy is the first ring of influence because any action taken by an individual starts with themselves. Individuals have **agency**, in other words, the ability to act independently and make choices. There is debate among social science researchers about how much influence **structures** have on one's agency, that is, factors in society that control choice making such as race, gender, religion, and social class (Gibbs, 2017). Nevertheless, the foundation of American democracy, written within the Declaration of Independence and the US Constitution, promotes an ideal of "free will." Every day, one can make choices that affect the direction of their life. Many of those choices are small, such as what to eat for lunch or whether to watch another episode on Netflix. Yet one also encounters larger, life-changing decisions, such as whether to go to college to become a teacher or to be in a relationship with a certain person.

Educators also have agency pertaining to many aspects of their profession. Whether you are in a classroom co-teaching, eating lunch with colleagues, attending school leadership meetings, or even outside of school talking with friends and family, each interaction provides an opportunity to influence others. The self-advocacy ring is about advocating for yourself to influence others for change—change to help you do your job; to better your working conditions; to support the profession of special education, which has transformed the lives of children with disabilities.

There is an old saying that goes "If you don't have a seat at the table, you're likely on the menu." Although constant paranoia about others "out to get you" is unhealthy, there is truth in the saying about being involved when decisions are made. Self-advocacy is important because without it, others are left to shape the **narrative** about your job and your needs. Allowing others to fill the void and discuss the needs and solutions of special education teachers is a precarious proposition. Besides, no one is more qualified to know your job and your needs than you!

Kaufman and Ring (2011) contend that teachers who confront and resolve professional obstacles through self-advocacy are better equipped to attend to the instructional, social, and emotional needs of their students. When teachers have the capacity to focus on the academic and social/emotional growth of their students, feelings of **self-efficacy** increase. And increased self-efficacy leads to higher job satisfaction (Zee et al., 2016). But only you can identify specific needs you have to improve your working conditions. As we discussed in chapter 2, problem identification is the first step in advocacy. One must recognize a problem and begin to understand causes of the problem before entering the next steps of advocacy, which are inviting relevant **stakeholders** to the conversation and then working on solutions to enact change. Although we cannot discuss every instance that may arise in the profession, in the next section, we identify several persistent problems in the profession that require self-advocacy skills. To answer the question of why advocate for yourself, the answer is quite simply because (1) only you know your needs, (2) you will enjoy your job more, and (3) your students will have better outcomes.

WHAT ARE SOME CURRENT OPPORTUNITIES FOR SELF-ADVOCACY?

In the next section of this chapter, we discuss several opportunities that special education teachers may encounter that require self-advocacy. Obviously, the issues presented are not an exhaustive list, yet they do represent persistent topics discussed in special education literature. In addition, each topic may have specific nuances depending on particular situations.

Curricular Resources

Access to current, evidence-based curricular resources is imperative for special education teachers to meet the instructional needs of their students. In fact, special education teachers rated access to adequate resources (including assistive technology) as the highest issue in terms of their own success as teachers (Fowler et al., 2019). When special education teachers are provided with curricular resources, such as textbooks, instructional materials, and scope and sequence plans, studies have shown they have less stress and are more likely to stay in the profession (Bettini et al., 2020). In contrast, when teachers do not have access to curricular resources, they are more likely to report high levels of stress and burnout with an increased desire to leave the job (Billingsley et al., 2020).

   Special education teachers can have a wide-ranging caseload with varying student needs. Without access to curricular resources, teachers often struggle with knowing what to teach, instead of focusing efforts on specially designed instruction and appropriate student supports (Billingsley & Bettini, 2017). Advocating for curricular resources is necessary because it reduces the time spent searching for and creating materials for instruction. Teachers can instead use that time planning for instruction and making decisions around individual student's needs. According to the Council of Exceptional Children code of ethics (CEC, 2022), special education teachers are responsible for "advocating for professional conditions and resources that will improve learning outcomes of individuals with exceptionalities." Advocating for the curricular resources needed to be effective will result in the greater likelihood of special educators staying in the field while concurrently leading to better outcomes for students (Bettini et al., 2020).

Role Definition

Special education teachers are responsible for a variety of roles as part of their profession. They lead individualized education program (IEP) teams to develop, implement, and monitor IEPs for every student on their caseload. Special education teachers often co-teach with general education colleagues, while also engaging in direct instruction throughout the day. They collaborate with parents, administrators, and other relevant stakeholders. In addition, special education teachers often support students with behavioral needs, which leads to added legal compliance responsibilities such as functional behavioral assessments (FBAs), positive behavior interventions and supports (PBIS) plans, and manifestation determinations. It is no surprise that with a myriad of roles and responsibilities, special education teachers feel overwhelmed and stressed. Self-advocacy is needed, therefore, to define roles, communicate expectations, and collaborate on solutions.

Inclusion

As more schools adopt inclusive practices, special education teachers are expected to provide services to students in general education settings. According to the US Department of Education (2019), the number of students with disabilities receiving their education in the general education classroom almost doubled, from 33% in 1990 to more than 62% in 2015. There is consistent evidence that inclusive educational settings can create substantial short- and long-term benefits for students with and without disabilities (Hehir et al., 2016). However, at the same time, special education teachers are required to consider the appropriateness of a student's special education services (i.e., free appropriate public education [FAPE]) over the student's least restrictive environment (LRE; Markelz & Bateman, 2022). Despite evidence to support inclusive practices and the social justice aspect of providing similar opportunities for all students, there remains logistical, philosophical, and educational hurdles that maintain segregated classrooms even when they are not most appropriate for the student (Murawski & Hughes, 2021). Guiding IEP team members toward decisions about students' educational services and their placement requires confidence and commitment.

Student Behavior

Challenging student behavior has been a common reported factor in teacher burnout (Hastings & Brown, 2002). Not only do undesirable student behaviors interrupt instruction; they also negatively affect teacher–student relationships. Teachers who struggle with classroom management issues report higher levels of anxiety and are more likely to leave the profession (Westling, 2010). Although special education teachers serve as case managers and oversee behavioral interventions through IEPs, supporting students with challenging behaviors is a shared responsibility among IEP team members. Too often, special education teachers find themselves reacting to disruptive behaviors and constantly putting out fires, as opposed to implementing proactive, collaborative strategies that reinforce appropriate behaviors (Maag, 2001; Markelz et al., 2020). Special education teachers should advocate for themselves to share the responsibilities of behavioral supports by working together with administrators, general education teachers, paraprofessionals, and families.

Special education teachers often have students on their caseloads who receive some or all of their instruction in general education classrooms. Unfortunately, students with behavioral needs in general education classrooms may receive more negative feedback than students without behavioral needs (Scott et al., 2017). Persistent undesirable student behaviors may prompt general education teachers to ask these students to go to a special education classroom. Thus, a divide is perpetuated between "general education students" and "special education students."

It is important for special education teachers to communicate to all IEP team members that just like academic interventions and accommodations, students are also entitled to behavioral supports to receive FAPE in their LRE. Special education teachers have knowledge and training in best practices regarding proactive classroom management strategies and should be confident in this knowledge. Supporting students with behavioral needs requires effective collaboration with all stakeholders across all settings (e.g., general education classrooms, extracurricular activities, home). Self-advocacy to collaborate on the development and implementation of PBIS will more effectively and efficiently provide students with the behavioral supports they require.

Professional Relationships

As IEP team case managers, special education teachers must preserve professional relationships to successfully perform their job. According to the Individuals with Disabilities Education Act (IDEA, 2004), required IEP team members are (a) the student's parents or legal guardian, (b) at least one special education teacher, (c) at least one general education teacher, (d) a representative from the local education agency that is qualified to provide or supervise the special education program (usually the school principal), and (e) the child (when appropriate). Other relevant stakeholders may serve on the IEP team (but are not required) such as those who provide related services. Although each member of the IEP team should want what is best for the student, those opinions are not always in sync. In fact, competing priorities, logistical issues, and differences in philosophy may hinder cooperative efforts to develop, implement, monitor, and adjust IEPs.

Successful relationships are built on a foundation of trust, mutual respect, and open communication (Cross & Parker, 2004). It is the responsibility of special education teachers to develop and maintain those relationships with administrators, general education teachers, and families. True, this can be a daunting and challenging task. Finding the time and energy to work with colleagues or families who appear skeptical, hesitant, or even hostile can be stressful. Therefore, special education teachers must remember to advocate for themselves to maintain healthy relationships. Special education teachers are called to the profession for many reasons, but it is clear that a strong desire exists to better the lives and outcomes of students with disabilities. In doing so, special education teachers may continually give more time, more effort, and more energy toward their students' needs without maintaining a personal–work life balance. Healthy professional relationships with all members of the IEP team require self-advocacy to communicate clear boundaries and expectations.

Special Education Teachers of Color

Teachers of color can improve academic and social outcomes for all students, as well as serve as role models, especially for students of color (Henfield, 2013; Redding, 2019). Yet special education teachers of color struggle to balance their professional responsibilities, such as instruction, with forced obligations. For example, special education teachers of color feel pressure to serve as racial experts, as racial justice advocates, and in nonacademic positions (e.g., disciplinarians, cultural and language interpreters, sports coaches) because they are stereotyped as having an interest or being skilled in these roles (Pabon, 2016).

Special education teachers of color have unique experiences and challenges for which self-advocacy is needed. Teachers of color may experience **institutional racism** throughout their careers, resulting in feelings of inequity or lack of belonging in their schools. For example, the only Black teacher in a school may feel like they do not belong when they are the only one fighting against racism for students. Institutional racism can include policies, practices, and procedures, as well as habits, attitudes, and behaviors of individuals, either intentional or unintentional (Howard, 2010).

In addition to systemic issues of racism in K–12 schools, teachers of color often experience **microaggressions**, which affect job satisfaction (DeCuir-Gunby & Gunby, 2016). Microaggressions are common, subtle, intentional—or unintentional—interactions that communicate some sort of bias toward a historically marginalized group. For example, a group of colleagues ask Mrs. Lopez (the only Hispanic teacher) to meet with a Latina student to discuss why the student has been frequently absent. Even though Mrs. Lopez barely knows the student, her colleagues believe that she will be able to better connect with the student because they share the same ethnicity. Special education teachers of color prepare and dedicate their careers to educate and advocate for students with disabilities. Once in schools, however, many find themselves in roles of also advocating specifically for students of color (Cormier et al., 2022). There are many challenges facing all special education teachers, but stressors of racial and cultural differences compound the difficulties for special education teachers of color. Self-advocacy is needed for teachers of color to navigate their school systems, make wise decisions, and collaborate with colleagues.

Workload Manageability

Special education teacher burnout and stress are leading reasons why teachers are leaving the profession at an alarming rate (Bettini et al., 2017). It seems like special education teachers are constantly being asked to do more with less. Unfortunately, persistent teacher shortages will only compound this problem because schools are forced to make tough decisions about providing legally compliant services under IDEA with fewer and fewer licensed special education teachers. The **caseload** size of a special education teacher has a major effect on their workload. Caseloads are determined at the state level, and each state has different requirements regarding caseload size. In a review of state caseload policies, Hogue and Taylor (2020) found that 20 states do not mention caseload policies within state special education legislation—two states did not respond to the study. Eight state policies mention caseload but no specifics about number requirements. For example, Indiana's caseload policy explains that "special education teachers' caseloads must be limited in order to allow the teacher to implement each student's IEP, determined by (a) the nature and severity of the student's disability, (b) the type and intensity of services required by the students, (c) the chronological ages of the students served, and (d) the total number of students both with and without disabilities on the teacher's caseload" (Indiana Special Education Rules [Article 7], 2019).

The remaining 20 states have specific caseload guidance policies; however, no two state policies are alike. For example, West Virginia policy states, "caseloads of students with developmental delays who are age 3-5 may have up to 20 students, while all other special education teacher caseloads may have up to 30 students" (West Virginia Department of Education, 2017). New Mexico has a caseload policy based on the percentage of a day a student spends in a special education classroom: "the maximum caseload for a special education teacher depends on the percentage of time that the students spend in special education; less than 10% of the school day (35); less than 50% of the school day (24); more than 50% of the school day (15); nearly the full day (8)" (New Mexico Public Education Department, 2022). Across the 20 states with specific policies, the mean number of maximum students per caseload was 31.56 (SD = 9.65; Hogue & Taylor, 2020).

Caseload sizes directly relate to the amount of work required by special education teachers. The addition of one student to a caseload significantly increases responsibilities in meetings, relationship building, collaboration, IEP monitoring and adjustment, and behavioral supports (if needed), let alone daily instruction and assessment duties. Unfortunately, administrators do not seem to understand the effect that caseloads have on special education teacher workloads. In a study by Hagaman and Casey (2018), novice special education teachers indicated that large and complex caseloads were one reason why they would leave the profession, yet administrators did not even list caseloads as a factor contributing to attrition.

Special education teachers need to self-advocate for realistic expectations considering caseload sizes and workload manageability—especially in states with ambiguous or no state policies. For too long, one short-term answer for teacher shortages has been to increase caseloads. However, decades of research indicate that this solution is potentially causing more teacher burnout and great numbers exiting the field (Billingsley & Bettini, 2019; Nichols & Sosnowsky, 2002; Russ et al., 2001).

In Summary

There are many reasons that you should advocate for yourself and the special education profession. In the previous section, we highlighted a few common issues that special education teachers frequently encounter that lead to greater stress, lack of resources, and a more challenging environment to do their job (table 3.1). Without a doubt, special education teachers' roles and responsibilities go beyond instruction for students with disabilities, but when teachers have time, resources, administrative support, and colleague cooperation, they can be more effective educators. Observing student progress can lead to feelings of self-efficacy, which can lead to higher job satisfaction (Zee et al., 2016). Simply put, when teachers are less stressed and more supported, they are better teachers, and better teachers lead to better student outcomes. As Congress stated in 1975 with the passage of IDEA, better student outcomes are the foundational purpose of special education.

> Improving educational results for children with disabilities is an essential element of our national policy of ensuring equality of opportunity, full participation, independent living, and economic self-sufficiency for individuals with disabilities. (Education for All Handicapped Children Act of 1975)

Table 3.1. Common Issues Facing Special Education Teachers

Issue	What is it?	Why self-advocate?
Curricular resources	Access to textbooks, instructional materials, assistive technologies, and scope and sequence plans that are aligned to the diverse instructional needs of all students on a caseload.	With appropriate curricular resources, less time is spent searching and creating materials. Instead, professional expertise is more efficiently used to specifically design instruction and make individualized educational decisions to improve student outcomes.
Professional roles	Special education teachers have many responsibilities beyond instructor. They are IEP team leaders, general educator and family collaborators, student advocates, inclusive practice experts, data collectors, and behavior management professionals.	Communicating expectations, defining boundaries, and sharing responsibilities to solve problems will create a healthy work–life balance. All stakeholders in a student's education will be working toward a singular goal.
Workload manageability	The time, resources, and support needed to successfully perform the job of special education teacher.	Unreasonable and unmanageable workloads lead to stress and teacher burnout. Special education teachers must advocate for the time, resources, and support to counter professional trends that continually ask teachers to do more with less.

The special education teacher shortage is not a new phenomenon (Billingsley, 2004). The immediacy of the problem, however, has been snowballing toward crisis-level shortages that districts are facing across the country. The COVID-19 pandemic only exacerbated this crisis. Rather than investing to attract, prepare, and retain quality special education teachers, local, state, and federal policies have consistently resorted to lowering the bar to entry. Unprepared and underexperienced teachers not only have poorer student outcomes but also are more likely to leave the profession, which continues the teacher shortage crisis (Billingsley & Bettini, 2017). We will discuss the teacher shortage crisis in more detail in chapter 9, yet for too long, the narrative has become that anybody can step into the role of special education teacher and be successful. To ensure the promise of IDEA that all students deserve equality of opportunity, that narrative must change. With self-advocacy, you can communicate that a successful special education teacher is highly knowledgeable, well trained, and specifically skilled at meeting the individual needs of students with disabilities.

HOW DO YOU ADVOCATE FOR YOURSELF?

It is common practice to teach students with disabilities self-advocacy skills to empower them with decision-making and increase their agency regarding postsecondary outcomes (Roberts et al., 2016). The same idea applies to special education teachers. Special education teachers who self-advocate will increase agency and empowerment to affect their abilities and job satisfaction. As identified in chapter 2, advocacy is about the following:

1. Identifying and understanding the problem
2. Inviting all stakeholders involved to listen to each other
3. Determining potential solutions to enact change

Applying these steps to one's individual circumstances is the key to self-advocacy (figure 3.2).

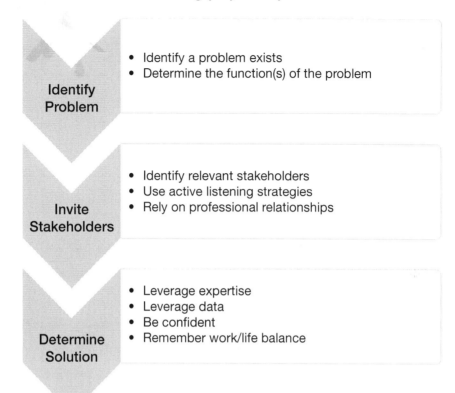

Figure 3.2.   How to Self-Advocate

Identify and Understand the Problem

In the previous section, we identified a few common problems that special education teachers encounter; however, self-advocacy can apply to any situation. From small problems to larger, more complex issues, the first step is to identify that a problem exists. This is generally an easy step. Beyond identifying that a problem exists, the next important step is to understand why the problem is occurring. In special education, we call this determining the **function of behavior**. Just as one would examine the function of a student's challenging behavior before developing an intervention to address that function, it is equally important that special education teachers begin to examine the root causes of a problem. After asking what the problem is, ask why the problem is occurring.

Understanding the causes of problems requires one to be proactive. Ask questions and seek clarification. It is also helpful to be open-minded about the contexts that are contributing to the problem. For example, are there circumstances that are out of your control? Are there other priorities that might be superseding what you deem to be the priority? As the old saying goes, "There are two sides to every story." Self-reflection is an essential skill when understanding problems because it allows one to examine the issue from their own point of view, but then it also allows examination outside their point of view. During this process, one should gather data (formally or informally) to inform their understanding of the problem and causes.

Invite Stakeholders

After the problem has been identified with a thorough consideration of the causes, it is time to invite all stakeholders to discuss the issue. As previously mentioned, self-advocacy is about advocating for yourself. But it is equally important to know to whom you are advocating. Understanding the problem allows one to better know who a relevant stakeholder is and who should be invited to discuss solutions. Depending on the issue, a relevant stakeholder may simply be a co-teacher. It may be a parent. It may be the principal and a parent. It may be the entire IEP team. It may be the school board. It may be state senators and representatives. Self-advocacy requires advocating for yourself to those who can contribute to solutions.

Good communication is an important part of professional relationships (Friend & Cook, 2016). Ineffective communication can lead to misunderstandings, wrong assumptions, and distrust. Having identified and done the work to understand the problem, one will be prepared to lead an informed discussion. When discussing the problem and root causes with relevant stakeholders, one should use active listening strategies to obtain a clear understanding of everyone's perspective.

McNaughton and Vostal (2010) developed a framework based on literature about effective communication. Although originally developed for communication with parents, the mnemonic is applicable to various active listening contexts (figure 3.3). The first part of the mnemonic (LAFF) represents steps involved in active listening. The first step (L) allows the stakeholder to share their perspective. The second step (A) involves learning more about the stakeholder's perspective through asking questions. Open-ended questions are particularly valuable to gather insight. During these meetings, it is important to focus on the issue (F) and not get derailed from the purpose, which is to discuss the identified problem. McNaughton and Vostal suggest that most problems benefit from gathering additional information and careful thought.

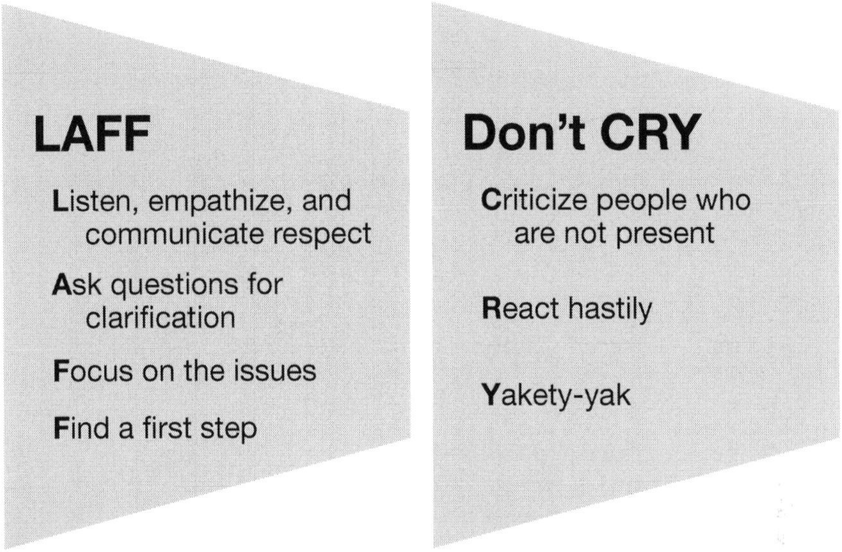

LAFF

Listen, empathize, and communicate respect

Ask questions for clarification

Focus on the issues

Find a first step

Don't CRY

Criticize people who are not present

React hastily

Yakety-yak

Figure 3.3. The LAFF Don't CRY Active Listening Strategy
Note. Developed by McNaughton and Vostal, 2010.

Therefore, meeting members are encouraged to find a first step (F) to begin moving in the right direction. Setting a target date for a follow-up meeting is recommended so that there is accountability to come back and discuss progress or ongoing concerns.

The second part of the framework (CRY) summarizes communication behaviors that are not helpful when having an open, respectful conversation (McNaughton & Vostal, 2010). Criticizing people who are not present (C) is unhelpful in gaining a greater understanding of the problem. If the discussion involves a person who is not present, perhaps that person is a relevant stakeholder and should be invited to the conversation to partake in a solution. One should also avoid reacting hastily (R) either out of self-defense or a desire to quickly solve the problem. Finally, in a stressful situation, many people talk to break the silence or lighten the mood. Limit yakety-yak (Y) conversations that derail the purpose and progress of active listening.

Given that special education teachers fill a variety of professional roles, they also must maintain multiple professional relationships. Positive professional relationships are important for many reasons such as school climate, better student outcomes, and job satisfaction (Cornelius & Gustafson, 2021), but they are also necessary for self-advocacy. Trust is a critical component when working with others to solve problems. Without the foundations of a healthy professional relationship, people may be unapproachable when invited to discuss an issue or dismissive of perspectives and experiences. Professional relationships are especially important when advocating to stakeholders at classroom- and school-level rings of influence because interactions with these individuals are most likely ongoing. However, as we will discuss in chapters 6 and 7, developing professional relationships with stakeholders at the state and federal rings of influence is crucial for successful advocacy at these levels as well.

Determine Solutions

Once a problem has been identified and understood and all stakeholders have had a chance to listen to each other's perspectives, it is time to determine a solution. Some solutions may be quick to identify and easy to implement. Others may be much more complex with no obvious solution that meets everyone's priorities. When self-advocating for a solution, we encourage special education teachers to leverage their expertise, leverage data, be confident, and remember professional role responsibilities and work–life balance.

Special education teachers are often humble about what they know and what they can do (Karten & Murawski, 2020). However, licensed special education teachers have the training and ongoing practice of unique knowledge and skills that members of an IEP team do not have. Even school administrators have minimal preparation in special education laws and policies (Sun & Xin, 2019). A special education teacher who relies on their professional training and understanding of the problem is able to leverage their expertise when self-advocating for a solution.

Just as special education teachers use data to monitor student progress and make instructional decisions, self-advocacy solutions should be grounded in evidence. A person who enters a meeting organized and prepared to present data will set the tone that they are a professional. The type of data is dependent on the problem. For example, to advocate for more planning time with your co-teachers, you could log daily activities on a spreadsheet, then convert those activities into charts or graphs to show how your time is spent throughout the day and week. It would then be easy to depict that the current schedule does not allocate sufficient time to meet the inclusive needs of students on your caseload. Without data, advocating for more planning time could simply be dismissed as a complaint by your administrator who might not be aware of all the activities you are responsible for throughout the week.

Special education teachers have substantial training and expertise in areas such as specially designed instruction (SDI), universal design for learning (UDL), behavior support, assistive technologies, family collaboration, high-leverage practices (Council for Exceptional Children, 2018), progress monitoring, and much more. When self-advocating for solutions, special education teachers should be confident in identifying the problem, the work done to understand the problem, and their knowledge and skills to solve the problem. Obviously, it is unhelpful to come off as a know-it-all, which is why active listening strategies are encouraged during discussions, but there is a distinction between prepared and confident and unprepared and arrogant.

Finally, when self-advocating for a solution, we encourage special education teachers to remember to maintain a work–life balance. Teacher burnout is a significant issue among special education teachers. The natural instinct of a special education teacher may be to do more, give more, and try harder, but without mental and physical well-being, **attrition** in the profession will continue. Advocating for self-care when determining solutions is integral in maintaining personal health.

WHERE CAN I FIND MORE INFORMATION ON SELF-ADVOCACY?

From the Field

 This blog from the Council for Exceptional Children (CEC) provides an outlet for articles for and by special education teachers and researchers. It is a great way to remain up to date on issues affecting teachers and learn about resources available to you through the CEC. To start reading, visit https://exceptional children.org/blog/category/field.

TEACHING Exceptional Children Special Issue on Self-Advocacy

 In this peer-reviewed journal for special education teachers, the authors of volume 53, issue 3, discuss multiple ways to self-advocate to confront and resolve professional obstacles. Several practical strategies are highlighted with real-life vignettes to facilitate implementation. Access the special issue at https://journals.sage pub.com/toc/tcxa/53/3.

Self-Advocacy: Improving Your Life by Speaking Up

 An informative blog post that presents critical elements, benefits, and resources for self-advocacy in an easy-to-read format. Visit https://www.betterup.com/blog/self-advocacy.

Speaking Up Is Hard to Do

 In this TED talk (15 minutes), social psychologist Adam Galinsky discusses how to assert yourself, navigate social situations, and expand your personal power. Visit https://www.youtube.com/watch?v=MEDgtjpycYg.

KEY TERMS

agency: Ability to act independently and make decisions.

attrition: Departure of employees from a profession.

caseload: The number of students with Individual Education Programs (IEPs) for whom a special education teacher serves as the "case manager" and is responsible for writing and implementing the IEP.

function of behavior: The reason why a behavior is occurring.

institutional racism: A form of racism that is embedded in the laws and regulations of a society or an organization; also known as systemic racism.

microaggressions: Common, subtle, intentional—or unintentional—interaction that communicates some sort of bias toward a historically marginalized group.

narrative: The telling of a story or events.

self-efficacy: The belief in one's abilities.

stakeholders: The people with an interest or concern in something.

structures: Factors in society that control or influence decision-making (either consciously or unconsciously).

DISCUSSION QUESTIONS

1. In your own words, why is self-advocacy important for special education teachers?
2. What are some obstacles special education teachers encounter that require self-advocacy?

3. What issues in your life could benefit from self-advocacy? Using steps from this chapter, how can you self-advocate for change?
4. How can self-advocacy influence the narrative about the special education profession?
5. Why should self-care be a consideration when self-advocating?

REFERENCES

Bettini, E., Gilmour, A. F., Williams, T. O., & Billingsley, B. (2020). Predicting special and general educators' intent to continue teaching using conservation of resources theory. *Exceptional Children*, *86*(3), 310–329. https://doi.org/10.1177/0014402919870464

Bettini, E., Jones, N., Brownell, M., Conroy, M., Park, Y., Leite, W., Crockett, J., & Benedict, A. (2017). Workload manageability among novice special and general education teachers: Relationships with emotional exhaustion and career intentions. *Remedial and Special Education*, *38*(4), 246–256. https://doi.org/10.1177/0741932517708327

Billingsley, B. S. (2004). Special education teacher retention and attrition: A critical analysis of the research literature. *Journal of Special Education*, *38*(1), 39–55. https://doi.org/10.1177%2F00224669040380010401

Billingsley, B., & Bettini, E. (2017). Improving special education teacher quality and effectiveness. In J. M. Kauffman, D. P. Hallahan, & P. C. Pullen (Eds.), *Handbook of special education* (pp. 501–520). Routledge. https://doi.org/10.4324/9781315517698-39

Billingsley, B., & Bettini, E. (2019). Special education teacher attrition and retention: A review of the literature. *Review of Educational Research*, *89*(5), 697–744. https://doi.org/10.3102%2F0034654319862495

Billingsley, B., Bettini, E., Mathews, H. M., & McLeskey, J. (2020). Improving working conditions to support special educators' effectiveness: A call for leadership. *Teacher Education and Special Education*, *43*(1), 7–27.

Cormier, C. J., Scott, L. A., Powell, C., & Hall, K. (2022). Locked in glass classrooms: Black male special education teachers socialized as everything but educators. *Teacher Education and Special Education*, *45*(1), 77–94. https://doi.org/10.1177/08884064211061038

Cornelius, K. E., & Gustafson, J. A. (2021). Relationships with school administrators: Leveraging knowledge and data to self-advocate. *TEACHING Exceptional Children*, *53*(3), 206–214. https://doi.org/10.1177%2F0040059920972438

Council for Exceptional Children. (2018). *High-leverage practices.* https://highleveragepractices.org/

Council for Exceptional Children. (2022). *What every special educator must know: Professional ethics & standards.*

Cross, R., & Parker, A. (2004). *The hidden power of social networks: Understanding how work really gets done in organizations.* Harvard Business School Press.

DeCuir-Gunby, J. T., & Gunby, N. W., Jr. (2016). Racial microaggressions in the work-place: A critical race analysis of the experiences of African American educators. *Urban Education, 51*(4), 390–414. https://doi.org/10.1177/0042085916628610

Education for All Handicapped Children Act of 1975, 20 U.S.C. § 1401.

Fowler, S. A., Coleman, M. R. B., & Bogdan, W. K. (2019). The state of the special education profession survey report. *TEACHING Exceptional Children, 52*(1), 8–29. https://doi.org/10.1177/0040059919875703

Friend, M., & Cook, L. (2016). *Interactions: Collaboration skills for school professionals* (7th ed.). Pearson.

Gibbs, B. J. (2017, August 21). Structuration theory. *Encyclopedia Britannica.* https://www.britannica.com/topic/structuration-theory

Hagaman, J. L., & Casey, K. J. (2018). Teacher attrition in special education: Perspectives from the field. *Teacher Education and Special Education, 41*(4), 277–291. https://doi.org/10.1177%2F0888406417725797

Hastings, R. P., & Brown, T. (2002). Coping strategies and the impact of challenging behaviors on special educators' burnout. *Mental Retardation, 40*, 148–156. https://doi.org/10.1352/0047-6765(2002)040<0148:CSATIO>2.0.CO;2

Hehir, T., Grindal, T., Freeman, B., Lamoreau, R., Borquaye, Y., & Burke, S. (2016). *A summary of the evidence on inclusive education.* ABT Associates. https://www.abtassociates.com/insights/publications/report/summary-of-the-evidence-on-inclusive-education

Henfield, M. S. (2013). Meeting the needs of gifted and high-achieving black males in urban schools. *The Urban Review, 45*(4), 395–398.

Hogue, L. B., & Taylor, S. S. (2020). A review of special education caseload policies state by state: What impact do they have? *Journal of Special Education Leadership, 33*(1), 25–35.

Howard, T. C. (2010). *Why race and culture matter in schools: Closing the achievement gap in America's classrooms.* Teachers College Press.

Indiana Special Education Rules, Ind. Admin. Code, Article 7 § 36.11. (2019).

Individuals with Disabilities Education Act of 2004, 20 U.S.C. § 1400.

Karten, T., & Murawski, W. W. (2020). *Co-teaching do's, don'ts, and do betters.* ASCD.

Kaufman, R. C., & Ring, M. (2011). Pathways to leadership and professional development: Inspiring novice special educators. *TEACHING Exceptional Children, 43*(5), 52–60.

Maag, J. W. (2001). Rewarded by punishment: Reflections on the disuse of positive reinforcement in schools. *Exceptional Children, 67*, 173–186. https://doi.org/10.1177/001440290106700203

Markelz, A. M., & Bateman, D. F. (2022). *The essentials of special education law.* Rowman & Littlefield.

Markelz, A., Scheeler, M. C., Riccomini, P., & Taylor, J. C. (2020). A systematic review of tactile prompting in teacher education. *Teacher Education and Special Education, 43*(4), 296–313. https://doi.org/10.1177%2F0888406419877500

McNaughton, D., & Vostal, B. R. (2010). Using active listening to improve collaboration with parents: The LAFF don't CRY strategy. *Intervention in School and Clinic, 45*(4), 251–256. https://doi.org/10.1177%2F1053451209353443

Murawski, W. W., & Hughes, C. E. (2021). Special educators in inclusive settings: Take steps for self-advocacy! *TEACHING Exceptional Children, 53*(3), 184–193. https://doi.org/10.1177%2F0040059920982263

New Mexico Public Education Department. (2022). *How to figure caseload maximums.* https://webnew.ped.state.nm.us/wp-content/uploads/2018/01/How-to-Figure-Caseload-Maximums-1.pdf

Nichols, A. S., & Sosnowsky, F. L. (2002). Burnout among special education teachers in self-contained cross-categorical classrooms. *Teacher Education and Special Education, 25*(1), 71–86. https://doi.org/10.1177%2F088840640202500108

Pabon, A. (2016). Waiting for Black Superman: A look at a problematic assumption. *Urban Education, 51*, 915–939. https://doi.org/10.1177%2F0042085914553673

Redding, C. (2019). A teacher like me: A review of the effect of student–teacher racial/ethnic matching on teacher perceptions of students and student academic and behavioral outcomes. *Review of Educational Research, 89*(4), 499–535. https://doi.org/10.3102%2F0034654319853545

Roberts, E. L., Ju, S., & Zhang, D. (2016). Review of practices that promote self-advocacy for students with disabilities. *Journal of Disability Policy Studies, 26*(4), 209–220. https://doi.org/10.1177%2F1044207314540213

Russ, S., Chiang, B., Rylance, B. J., & Bongers, J. (2001). Caseload in special education: An integration of research findings. *Exceptional Children, 67*(2), 161–172. https://doi.org/10.1177%2F001440290106700202

Scott, T. M., Hirn, R., & Cooper, J. (2017). *Teacher and student behaviors: Keys to success in classroom instruction.* Rowman & Littlefield.

Sun, A. Q., & Xin, J. F. (2019). School principals' opinions about special education services. *Preventing School Failure: Alternative Education for Children and Youth, 64*(2), 105–115. https://doi.org/10.1080/1045988X.2019.1681354

US Department of Education. (2019). *Digest of education statistics, 2017* (NCES 2018-070).

West Virginia Department of Education. (2017). *Policy 2419: Regulations for the education of students with exceptionalities.*

Westling, D. L. (2010). Teachers and challenging behaviors: Knowledge, views, and practices. *Remedial and Special Education, 31*, 48–63. https://doi.org/10.1177/0741932508327466

Zee, M., Koomen, H. M., Jellesma, F. C., Geerlings, J., & de Jong, P. F. (2016). Inter- and intra-individual differences in teachers' self-efficacy: A multilevel factor exploration. *Journal of School Psychology, 55*, 39–56. https://doi.org/10.1016/j.jsp.2015.12.003

Chapter Four

Ring of Classroom Advocacy

Improving the learning environment for all students within a classroom is the guiding principle behind classroom advocacy. As a classroom teacher or teacher with a full caseload of students you are uniquely qualified to understand the needs of your students within an academic setting. You have the opportunity to observe and interact with students individually and in whole-group settings. These frequent interactions provide you with insights regarding individual and whole-class needs. Additionally—and this will come as no surprise—your students need to learn to identify and express their own needs. The ability to express oneself to advocate for personal needs requires a set of skills that are not necessarily self-evident for students with disabilities. Students should be able to persevere in their learning, accurately evaluate their needs, and articulate those needs in an appropriate manner to the correct person at the correct time. As special educators, you can help students with disabilities navigate this process as you yourself engage in advocacy at the classroom level. In this chapter, we will explore the classroom advocacy ring as we begin to expand the five rings of advocacy (figure 4.1). In chapter 4, we will answer these essential questions:

1. What is the classroom advocacy ring and why is it important?
2. What are some current opportunities for classroom advocacy?
3. How do you advocate for students in your classroom?
4. Where can I find more information on classroom advocacy?

Figure 4.1. The Classroom Advocacy Ring

WHAT IS THE CLASSROOM ADVOCACY RING AND WHY IS IT IMPORTANT?

Classroom advocacy is an important part of the role of the special education teacher. The Council for Exceptional Children (CEC)—the nation's leading professional organization in support of special education and individuals with disabilities—recently published practice standards as guidance for special educators to improve the experiences of individuals with disabilities (Berlinghoff & McLaughlin, 2022). The first professional standard states that special educators will "advocate for improved outcomes for individuals with exceptionalities and their families" (CEC, 2020). In addition, CEC also lists professional ethical principles that special educators should be committed to uphold. Some of these ethical principles include the following:

- Maintaining challenging expectations for individuals with exceptionalities to develop the highest possible learning outcomes and quality of life potential in ways that respect their dignity, culture, language, and background.
- Maintaining a high level of professional competence and integrity and exercising professional judgment to benefit individuals with exceptionalities and their families.
- Promoting meaningful and inclusive participation of individuals with exceptionalities in their schools and communities.
- Developing relationships with families based on mutual respect and actively involving families and individuals with exceptionalities in educational decision-making.

- Using evidence, instructional data, research, and professional knowledge to inform practice.
- Advocating for professional conditions and resources that will improve learning outcomes of individuals with exceptionalities.

Moving from the self-advocacy ring (see chapter 3) to the classroom advocacy ring, it is important to identify a distinction between *for* whom you are advocating and *to* whom you are advocating. Although the self-advocacy ring was about advocating *for* yourself *to* a variety of stakeholders, the classroom advocacy ring brings in additional stakeholders *for* whom you can advocate—such as a particular student, a group of students, or all the students on your caseload.

Knowing that special educators are called to advocate for classrooms and caseloads, depending on the need, teachers may be advocating to other education professionals, building leaders, or families to improve the educational experience of their students. This type of advocacy is considered to be an essential part of being a professional in the education field. Special educators serve as an **ally** for students in their classroom, or someone who leverages access or resources to advocate for a group or individuals without being part of the group. In this capacity, special educators work to identify and secure resources and solutions for classroom and caseload needs.

There are countless instances in which one may have to advocate to colleagues, leaders, and family members to help accomplish improved learning experiences for students. This can include seeking service provisions, such as modifications and accommodations, during instruction and assessments for your students from your general education colleagues. Classroom advocacy can also include seeking classroom supplies or curricular resources from school leaders that will improve access to sustained learning such as level textbooks, extra sets of math manipulatives, or materials to create differentiated learning stations. Classroom advocacy may require seeking solutions for one student such as inclusion in general education classes or a whole group such as inclusion in grade-level field trips. It can also mean brokering exchanges between parties such as helping families request student evaluations from the psychologist or working with the cafeteria staff and school principal on a seating plan that allows your students to be integrated and included while eating lunch with their nondisabled peers. Finally, classroom advocacy may also require special education teachers to help students with disabilities build their own capacity for self-advocacy through **co-advocacy** (Athanases & De Oliveira, 2008). Taken together, classroom advocacy depends on the needs of your classroom and the individual students within your classroom and requires a great deal of interpersonal relationship building.

WHAT ARE SOME CURRENT OPPORTUNITIES
FOR CLASSROOM ADVOCACY?

Working closely with students is why most teachers get into the education profession. And teachers have a direct effect on student outcomes within their own classroom. Yet as discussed in chapter 3, special educators are responsible for a variety of roles as part of their profession. When thinking about a list of opportunities for classroom advocacy, the instructional settings in which one educates play a significant factor. For example, special education teachers in a **self-contained** classroom will likely encounter some different advocacy opportunities for their students compared to special education teachers who **push in** to general education classrooms throughout the day. Regardless of these differences or where on the least restrictive environment (LRE) continuum one teaches, there are common best educational practices that all students deserve.

Instructional Best Practices

Educating students with disabilities requires teachers to use instructional practices that are more likely to positively affect their educational outcomes (Individuals with Disabilities Education Act [IDEA], 2004; Every Student Succeeds Act of 2015, 2015). However, educators often use strategies or promote practices that they have seen or heard other teachers use without questioning whether these practices are supported by evidence—the persistent misconception that students have unique "learning styles" comes to mind (Goodwin, 2021; Khazan, 2018). To improve the quality of instruction that students receive and the outcomes that students achieve, the field of education has been striving toward establishing educational practices that are supported by rigorous research. Given the importance of instructional practices, it is evident that special education teachers should advocate for their students to be instructed with methods that are most likely to increase their educational attainment.

Evidence-Based Practices

Evidence-based practices (EBPs) are skills, techniques, and strategies that have been consistently supported through experimental research studies or large-scale research field studies (IRIS Center, 2014). Depending on the skill being taught (e.g., reading fluency, fraction multiplication, social engagement), it is preferred that students be taught these skills using instructional practices that are supported by scientific evidence. Some examples of EBPs across a variety of subjects and skills are presented in table 4.1.

Table 4.1. **Evidence-Based Practices across Subjects**

Subject	Evidence-Based Practice	Research Summary
Reading and literacy	Accelerated Reader™: Adolescent Literacy	http://ies.ed.gov/ncee/wwc// InterventionReport/14
	Alphabetic Phonics: Students with a Specific Learning Disability	http://ies.ed.gov/ncee/wwc/ EvidenceSnapshot/26
	Book Clubs: Adolescent Literacy	http://www.ies.ed.gov/ncee/wwc/ EvidenceSnapshot/49
	ClassWide Peer Tutoring: Beginning Reading	http://ies.ed.gov/ncee/wwc/ EvidenceSnapshot/81
	Dialogic Reading: Early Childhood Education for Children with Disabilities	http://ies.ed.gov/ncee/wwc/ EvidenceSnapshot/136
	Dyslexia Training Program	https://ies.ed.gov/ncee/wwc/ EvidenceSnapshot/155
	Improving Adolescent Literacy: Effective Classroom and Intervention Practices	http://ies.ed.gov/ncee/wwc/Practice Guide.aspx?sid=8
	Reciprocal Teaching: Adolescent Literacy	http://ies.ed.gov/ncee/wwc/ EvidenceSnapshot/434
	Repeated Reading: Students with a Specific Learning Disability	http://ies.ed.gov/ncee/wwc/ EvidenceSnapshot/576
	Shared Book Reading: Early Childhood Education	http://ies.ed.gov/ncee/wwc/ EvidenceSnapshot/458
	Unbranded Orton-Gillingham-based Interventions: Students with a Specific Learning Disability	http://ies.ed.gov/ncee/wwc/ EvidenceSnapshot/528
Mathematics	Peer-Assisted Learning Strategies: Elementary School Mathematics	http://ies.ed.gov/ncee/wwc/ EvidenceSnapshot/619
	Improving Mathematical Problem Solving in Grades 4 Through 8	http://ies.ed.gov/ncee/wwc/Practice Guide.aspx?sid=16
	enVisionMATH: Primary Mathematics	http://ies.ed.gov/ncee/wwc/ EvidenceSnapshot/618
	Teaching Math to Young Children	http://ies.ed.gov/ncee/wwc/Practice Guide.aspx?sid=18
	The Expert Mathematician: Middle School Math	http://ies.ed.gov/ncee/wwc/ EvidenceSnapshot/513
	Building Decision Skills: Character Education	http://ies.ed.gov/ncee/wwc/ EvidenceSnapshot/61
Social skills and behavior	Connect with Kids: Character Education	http://ies.ed.gov/ncee/wwc/ EvidenceSnapshot/104
	Coping Power: Children Identified with or at Risk for an Emotional Disturbance	http://ies.ed.gov/ncee/wwc/ EvidenceSnapshot/588
	Social Skills Training: Early Childhood Education for Children with Disabilities	http://ies.ed.gov/ncee/wwc/ EvidenceSnapshot/578
	Too Good for Drugs and Violence (TGFD & V): Character Education	http://ies.ed.gov/ncee/wwc/ EvidenceSnapshot/516

While the research community is diligently identifying EBPs to improve special educators' practices and the outcomes of students with disabilities, not all academic and social skills or instructional strategies have been examined through research. This does not mean these instructional practices are not effective and should not be used. However, it does mean educators should implement certain strategies with caution and **progress monitor** to ensure students are benefiting from the instruction. EBPs may be the gold standard of instructional practices, but there are other classifications of practice that one should know. A promising practice is shown to have positive effects on student outcomes, but the research design does not clearly demonstrate a **functional relation** or there are too few studies to confirm the effect. A research-based practice has research support that demonstrates some positive effect on student outcomes while other research does not. These practices are ambiguous in whether there is evidence in support of the practice. An emerging practice is based on anecdotal evidence that has not undergone scientific experimentation.

If students on your caseload were instructed by a variety of teachers, wouldn't you want them exposed to teaching methods that are more effective than not? It may be unreasonable to advocate that all students be taught with EBPs all the time; however, as an ally for your students, you should advocate that they are instructed in practices that are more likely to help them succeed.

Although EBPs are desired when implementing specific instructional strategies, there is growing support for a framework to improve and optimize teaching and learning for all people based on scientific insights into how humans learn.

Universal Design for Learning

Just as the goal of the Americans with Disabilities Act (1990) was to make buildings physically accessible to all people, the goal of universal design for learning (UDL) is to make the classroom and learning accessible to all people. UDL emphasizes a variety of teaching methods to remove barriers to learning and give all students equal opportunities to succeed. There are three main principles to UDL (CAST, 2022).

Engagement is the first principle of UDL, and it addresses the "why" of learning. Some students may seem naturally engaged or motivated to learn, while others are disengaged and resistant. There are multiple influencing factors that affect students' motivation, including personal interests, background knowledge, learning history, physical condition (e.g., hungry or sick), and personal relationship with the teacher. Some students are highly engaged by spontaneity and novelty in the classroom, while others are frightened by those aspects and prefer strict routine. Some learners might like to work alone, while others prefer to work with their peers. The engagement principle of UDL recognizes that no single means of engagement will be optimal for all learners in all contexts; therefore, educators should provide multiple options for engagement to meet the needs of all learners.

The second principle of UDL is representation, and it addresses the "what" of learning. All students differ in the ways they perceive and comprehend information that is presented to them. For example, students with sensory disabilities (e.g., blindness or deafness) or learning disabilities (e.g., dyslexia) may require different ways of approaching content. Some students may grasp information more quickly with printed text than others who require visual and auditory instruction to comprehend the same material. UDL recognizes that students process content differently and that multiple means of representation likely strengthen students' abilities to make connections between concepts and learn content more effectively.

The third principle of UDL is action and expression, and it addresses the "how" of learning. In other words, how do students demonstrate their knowledge and skills of the content they were engaged in that the teacher represented? All students with significant movement impairments (e.g., cerebral palsy), who struggle with strategic and organizational abilities (e.g., executive function disorders), or who have language barriers approach learning tasks differently. These students will need to show their learning in a variety of ways. Multiple means of action and expression remove particular barriers that prevent students from demonstrating their knowledge. UDL encourages educators to expand on any **preconceived** notion of what formal or informal assessments should look like.

Multitiered Systems of Support

All educators, including special educators, should be familiar with multitiered systems of support (MTSS). Many schools use the MTSS framework to provide targeted support for students who are struggling academically and/or behaviorally. The goal of MTSS is to provide early intervention so students do not keep falling further behind their peers. Instead of the **waiting to fail** assessment model, MTSS takes a proactive approach to identifying students with academic or behavioral needs. MTSS is actually a combination of two other tiered systems of support that educators should be familiar with: response to intervention (RTI) and positive behavioral interventions and support (PBIS).

RTI is a tiered system of support that targets students' academic needs. It is also the model for identifying students with specific learning disabilities

(Markelz & Bateman, 2022). PBIS is a schoolwide approach to promote school safety and good behavior. The focus of PBIS is to prevent undesirable behaviors as opposed to solely relying on punishment procedures. MTSS is a combination of RTI and PBIS with these key elements:

- Universal screening for all students early in each school year.
- Increasing levels of targeted support through tiers of intervention for students who are struggling.
- Integrated plans that address students' academic, behavioral, social, and emotional needs.
- A schoolwide approach to student support that includes teachers, counselors, psychologists, and other specialists as needed.
- Professional development so teams can provide interventions and monitor progress effectively.
- Family involvement so parents and caregivers can understand the interventions and give support at home.
- Frequent monitoring of students' progress to help decide if they need more interventions.
- The use of EBPs at every tier of support.

Although MTSS is designed for early intervention to support students quickly, it can also help schools identify students who have not received adequate instruction versus those who truly have a disability and need special education services. Students who go through MTSS without improvements in their educational outcomes will come to the special education evaluation process with lots of documentation that can be helpful with developing their individualized education program (IEP). Advocating for a comprehensive MTSS model will benefit all students, including those with disabilities or those yet to be identified as needing special education.

IEP Legal Compliance

Clearly a major role for special education teachers is the development, implementation, and progress monitoring of students' IEPs. Special education teachers serve as the leader of the **IEP team** and must ensure IEPs are being implemented as written. This task may become more challenging with large caseloads of students who spend all or a majority of their time in general education classrooms. Are **accommodations** and **modifications** in the curriculum occurring? Are positive behavior intervention plans being followed? Are students receiving appropriate differentiation to access the general curriculum? Are students' IEPs reasonably calculated for them to make appropriate progress given their individual circumstances? Are students being educated in the LRE for them to receive free appropriate public education? These are just a few questions a special education teacher might ask as their students are educated in a variety of settings by a variety of school personnel. If the answer to any of these questions is no, then advocacy skills are needed to remedy any situation and ensure IEP legal compliance.

Free Appropriate Public Education

It is estimated that 85% to 90% of all special education litigation relates to free appropriate public education (FAPE) violations (Rozalski et al., 2021). As discussed in chapter 2, FAPE is the central gear of the IDEA (2004). Procedural and substantive requirements of FAPE can only be determined by the *Rowley/Endrew* two-part test set by the Supreme Court (*Endrew F. v. Douglas County School District*, 2017):

1. Has the school district complied with the procedures of the IDEA?
2. Is the IEP reasonably calculated to enable the student to make appropriate progress in light of the student's circumstances?

It is the job of special education teachers to ensure their students are receiving FAPE. This means their students are receiving specially designed instruction based on needs identified within the present levels of academic and functional performance statements. In addition, students must be making appropriate progress toward annual goals and objectives in light of their circumstances. Knowing your students' strengths and areas of need is critical in determining FAPE because how else can an IEP be reasonably calculated without knowing the "students' circumstances"? As the students' special education teacher and caseload manager, you may need to advocate for a change or increase in services, additional accommodations, or even a change in placement. Once an IEP has been developed, its implementation is not static. The key to a "reasonably calculated" IEP is that student progress is constantly being monitored. If the plan is working and the student is making progress, great! If not, the IEP team needs to meet and make adjustments.

Least Restrictive Environment

If students are not making appropriate progress in light of their circumstances, one adjustment to the IEP might be a change in placement. Current statutory and regulatory laws state that schools must ensure the following:

To the maximum extent appropriate, children with disabilities, including children in public or private institutions or other care facilities, are educated with children who are non-disabled; and special classes, separate schooling, or other removal of children with disabilities from the regular educational environment occurs only if the nature or severity of the disability is such that education in regular classes with the use of supplementary aids and services cannot be achieved satisfactorily. (IDEA, 2004)

Issues of **inclusion** and interpretations of least restrictive environment (LRE) have sparked an ongoing debate in special education (Kauffman, Anastasiou, et al., 2022). The specifics of this debate will be discussed in greater detail in chapter 8; however, special educators should be aware that philosophical positions are forming around the concept of LRE. Proponents of the full inclusion movement advocate for the removal of a continuum of placements and suggest that all students with any disability should be educated in the regular education classroom alongside their nondisabled peers (e.g., Slee, 2018; Taylor, 2016). Proponents of current IDEA laws and regulatory policy maintain that a continuum of placements is essential to meeting the individual needs of all students (e.g., Kauffman, Burke, et al., 2022). Scholars who defend this position also refer to case laws (e.g., *Endrew F.*) that have established the priority of FAPE over LRE when determining appropriate special education services (e.g., Yell & Prince, 2022).

Regardless of which position one takes within this debate, the decision about placement concerning students' special education programming is a team decision. Advocacy skills will be needed to keep the IEP team's focus on the students' best interests. After all, the whole purpose of special education is to provide students with disabilities educational opportunities. Advocating for students on your caseload to be placed where they can most likely succeed should remain at the forefront of everyone's mind.

Self-Advocacy through Co-Advocacy

Helping students become "agents of their own success" (National Center for Learning Disabilities, 2018) through self-advocacy and choice making is critically important for students with disabilities within and beyond the classroom. Recognizing needs, expressing those needs, setting goals and making choices to address needs, and accepting the outcomes of such choices are skills vital to success. Ultimately, students who are skilled in self-advocacy and choice making are better equipped to engage as contributing members of society in school, community, and work (Nagro et al., 2019; National Center for Learning Disabilities, 2018). Unfortunately, these skills do not always come naturally to students with disabilities. There are many instances where students are expected to speak for themselves but may be too apprehensive because they do not know how to communicate their needs. You can work with students to improve the learning environment and build self-advocacy and choice-making skills.

Consider the following scenario. You have a student with a disability who has an accommodation on his IEP that provides him with written notes for all classes. His social studies teacher was providing these notes but got COVID and has been absent for an entire week. The substitute teacher has not provided any notes, and there is an upcoming test. This student comes to you as his special education teacher. He asks you to get him the missing notes. This is an opportunity to help this student work on self-advocacy through co-advocacy. You provide this student with positive feedback since he came to you recognizing and expressing a need. You then offer to help the student think through possible solutions. Together, you discuss his options to ask a friend for a copy of the notes, ask the substitute teacher for the notes, or ask for permission to wait for the social studies teacher to return to take the test. You ask the student for pros and cons of each choice, contribute during this exercise as needed, and allow the student to settle on his preferred pathway forward. The student says he wants to ask the substitute teacher for the notes but is nervous to do so because he does not know if the teacher is aware of his IEP. In response, you offer to go with the student to speak with the substitute teacher about accessing class notes at the end of the day.

During lunch, you take a few minutes to stop by the substitute teacher's room. You introduce yourself and share that you are working with this particular student on many goals including self-advocacy. You briefly share some details with the substitute teacher. She explains that she did receive copies of the notes but did not know what to do with them. You mention there are multiple students who should be receiving the notes including the student who shared his concerns. Finally, you ask if it would be okay to come by with the student at the end of the day. You meet up with your student and walk to the substitute's classroom together. You review with your student and allow him to practice what he wants to say. Finally, you support your student during the exchange but let him lead the conversation. In this example, you advocated on behalf of this student and some of his classmates as well as supported the student in self-advocacy. This form of co-advocacy can (a) help build understanding of a situation among involved parties, (b) create a low-stakes yet authentic opportunity for students to practice, (c) create viable pathways to address current issues, and (d) help to build student confidence. Recognizing opportunities to find current solutions and build future skills is an excellent reason to co-advocate.

HOW DO YOU ADVOCATE FOR STUDENTS
IN YOUR CLASSROOM?

Whitby and colleagues (2013) shared suggestions for engaging in classroom advocacy that minimize potential discomfort including (a) being knowledgeable, (b) prioritizing students' needs, (c) developing respectful relationships with co-workers, (d) using diplomacy, and (e) always maintaining professionalism. Whitby and colleagues went on to provide strategies for classroom advocacy that include concrete steps for supporting students with disabilities. Figure 4.2 includes an adapted version of these strategies with examples to

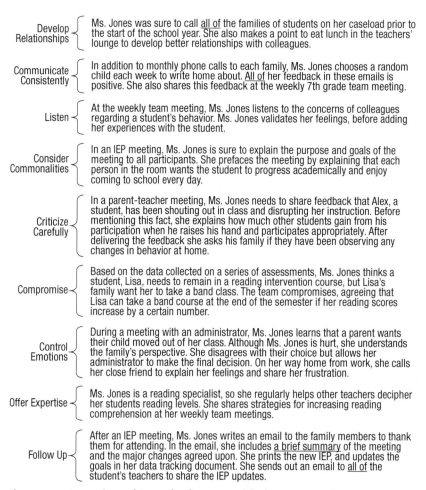

Develop Relationships	Ms. Jones was sure to call <u>all of</u> the families of students on her caseload prior to the start of the school year. She also makes a point to eat lunch in the teachers' lounge to develop better relationships with colleagues.
Communicate Consistently	In addition to monthly phone calls to each family, Ms. Jones chooses a random child each week to write home about. <u>All of</u> her feedback in these emails is positive. She also shares this feedback at the weekly 7th grade team meeting.
Listen	At the weekly team meeting, Ms. Jones listens to the concerns of colleagues regarding a student's behavior. Ms. Jones validates her feelings, before adding her experiences with the student.
Consider Commonalities	In an IEP meeting, Ms. Jones is sure to explain the purpose and goals of the meeting to all participants. She prefaces the meeting by explaining that each person in the room wants the student to progress academically and enjoy coming to school every day.
Criticize Carefully	In a parent-teacher meeting, Ms. Jones needs to share feedback that Alex, a student, has been shouting out in class and disrupting her instruction. Before mentioning this fact, she explains how much other students gain from his participation when he raises his hand and participates appropriately. After delivering the feedback she asks his family if they have been observing any changes in behavior at home.
Compromise	Based on the data collected on a series of assessments, Ms. Jones thinks a student, Lisa, needs to remain in a reading intervention course, but Lisa's family want her to take a band class. The team compromises, agreeing that Lisa can take a band course at the end of the semester if her reading scores increase by a certain number.
Control Emotions	During a meeting with an administrator, Ms. Jones learns that a parent wants their child moved out of her class. Although Ms. Jones is hurt, she understands the family's perspective. She disagrees with their choice but allows her administrator to make the final decision. On her way home from work, she calls her close friend to explain her feelings and share her frustration.
Offer Expertise	Ms. Jones is a reading specialist, so she regularly helps other teachers decipher her students reading levels. She shares strategies for increasing reading comprehension at her weekly team meetings.
Follow Up	After an IEP meeting, Ms. Jones writes an email to the family members to thank them for attending. In the email, she includes <u>a brief summary</u> of the meeting and the major changes agreed upon. She prints the new IEP, and updates the goals in her data tracking document. She sends out an email to <u>all of</u> the student's teachers to share the IEP updates.

Figure 4.2.   Strategies and Examples for Successful Classroom-Level Advocacy

Note. Adapted from "Advocating for students with disabilities at the school level: Tips for special educators," by Whitby, T. Marx, J. McIntire, and W. Wienke, 2013, *Teaching Exceptional Children,* 45(5), pp. 32–39.

illustrate how such strategies will be helpful during everyday life as a special education teacher. In the sections below, we will explain how these strategies come together.

Identify and Understand the Problem

Special educators who take a genuine interest in their students' development, their students' individual needs, and the collective needs of the classroom will become aware of a range of opportunities to advocate at the classroom level. In addition to looking inward toward students within the classroom, understand that problems also require an awareness of what is happening in the field of special education more broadly. Keeping current on EBPs, knowledge and skills around collaborative practices, **high-leverage practices**, and current trends in curriculum and instruction is an important aspect of understanding when something is problematic. In other words, use high standards as a ruler by which to measure the classroom rather than defaulting to a comparison of what has always been or what seems like the path of least resistance. This level of expertise requires an investment in ongoing professional development.

Keeping up to date on best practices will promote self-assurance and clarity as well as reduce uncertainty related to identifying opportunities for improving the learning experiences of students with disabilities across classroom settings (Nelson et al., 2022). One way to remain informed is to maintain active membership in national, state, or regional professional organizations such as the CEC, which publishes standards for practice, specialization skill sets, a code of ethics and professionalism, and research on all of the above. Such organizations often publish **research-to-practice journals**, which provide key insights into current educational practices. Maintaining a sense of understanding around special education best practices and special education law will help any special educator advocate from a position of knowledge and strength.

Invite Stakeholders

Once problems are identified and understood, the next step is to establish where solutions can be sought by identifying stakeholders. Speaking with colleagues, administrators, and families to understand multiple perspectives can help with identifying new solutions to ongoing challenges. This requires prioritizing time to connect with colleagues and setting norms for communication. For example, regularly occurring and structured meetings with written notes are a good way to share updates with your colleagues and set the expectation that communication will be ongoing and reciprocal. Similarly, regularly communicating with families to discuss student needs and share student progress encourages **reciprocal school–family partnerships**. During these sessions, it is helpful to include positive feedback whenever possible and use open-ended questions (e.g., "Can you tell me about . . . ?") to provide opportunities for families to detail insights that may be helpful when identifying problems or determining solutions (Francis et al., 2017). Maybe the most important part of seeking multiple perspectives is listening with the goal of understanding. Affirming what colleagues and families are saying before adding your own thoughts helps reinforce the shared responsibilities related to meeting student needs. Finally, after considering commonalities, criticizing carefully, compromising, deciding on what is nonnegotiable, and controlling your emotions, it is time to offer expertise and determine solutions. Being positive and upbeat while at the same time getting others involved will help stakeholders **coalesce** around a plan of action.

Determine Solutions

Special educators who understand their skill set, offer their expertise, focus on facts, and use data rather than opinions to drive actions will be well positioned to secure access and supports for their students and classroom. Whether making decisions about advocating for an individual student or the special needs of all students on your caseload, maintaining a student-centered, data-based focus will assure strong footing when entering into an advocacy opportunity.

Once armed with one or more potential solutions, it is time for effective communication to help gain traction. This requires a time investment, commitment to the improvement process, and an openness to change. For example, as parents are becoming increasingly involved with school board meetings, board members may place demands on classroom teachers about the use of certain curriculums. Teachers' responses will need to be clear and targeted to the specific needs of the students they serve, and teachers must work to ensure any curricular demands address the students' needs.

After coming to an agreement on a solution, be sure to reiterate the consensus reached by stakeholders. Restating the agreement can be easily done via an email or phone call. This may seem redundant, but it is important to ensure that each stakeholder is leaving the meeting with the same understanding of what was accomplished and agreed to. Thank families for their time, and be sure to follow through on any agreements you made. Following through with and thanking those who contributed to solutions will go a long way to maintaining those critical relationships and partnerships. Finally, track improvements and share those findings. When advocacy is successful, such successes should be celebrated and shared widely. Other educators need to see that pathways forward toward improved classroom outcomes are attainable. Building on incremental successes is a great way to make way for new solutions.

WHERE CAN I FIND MORE INFORMATION ON CLASSROOM ADVOCACY?

Evidence-Based Practices IRIS Module

 This interactive module from the IRIS Center at Vanderbilt University defines EBPs, explains why you should use them, and provides EBP resources by instructional level. Access this valuable resource at https://iris.peabody.vanderbilt.edu/ module/ebp_01/#content.

Response to Intervention: Collaborating to Target Instruction

 This YouTube video by Edutopia highlights how teachers implement RTI in a Michigan elementary school. Visit https:// www.youtube.com/watch?v=cpPZjcFw7xc.

Universal Design for Learning Guidelines

 CAST produced a straightforward and informative list of UDL guidelines that can be used by educators, curriculum developers, researchers, parents, or anyone else looking to learn more. Visit https://udlguidelines.cast.org/.

Universal Design for Learning IRIS Module

 This interactive module from the IRIS Center at Vanderbilt University explains the three principles of UDL. At the end of it, you should know how to apply these principles to the four curricular components: goals, instructional materials, instructional methods, and assessments. To get started, visit https://iris.peabody .vanderbilt.edu/module/udl/.

What Is MTSS? A Blog Post

 This blog post written by Jamie Harris, Ed.S., and published by Illuminate Education explains MTSS in detail and describes how districts implement this framework. Start reading at https://www.illuminateed.com/blog/2020/01/what-is-mtss-education/.

KEY TERMS

accommodations: Adjustments to instruction, materials, or environmental factors that allow a student with a disability to access the curriculum and demonstrate learning.

ally: Someone who leverages access or resources to advocate for a group or individuals without being part of the group.

co-advocacy: Helping students with disabilities build their own capacity for self-advocacy while advocating on their behalf.

coalesce: Coming together to form a unified group.

evidence-based practices: Skills, techniques, and strategies that have been consistently supported through the best evidence available from experimental research studies or large-scale research field studies.

functional relation: When the manipulation of an independent variable has an observable effect on the dependent variable.

high-leverage practices: A set of knowledge and skills that every K–12 special education teacher should master and be able to demonstrate.

IEP team: Consists of a parent or guardian, one regular education teacher, one special education teacher, a school administrator, an individual who can interpret student evaluation data, and the child when appropriate.

inclusion: The action or state of students with disabilities being part of a group that includes nondisabled peers.

modifications: Change in the curriculum that can include a reduction or change to the content targeted, process for learning, or ways students demonstrate understanding.

preconceived: An idea or opinion formed before having the evidence to determine its truthfulness.

progress monitor: Frequent, ongoing assessment of students' progress toward stated goals.

push in: Special education teachers bring necessary resources and materials to the students in their classroom setting to allow them to engage in learning.

reciprocal school–family partnerships: Partnerships where families and educators share common goals, see each other as equals, and support the students' education through ongoing two-way communication.

research-to-practice journals: Publications that provide key insights from research findings translated into actionable steps for practitioners.

self-contained: A classroom in which all the students have IEPs and a special education teacher is responsible for all instruction.

waiting to fail: A model where referrals for additional instruction or educational supports are provided only after a documented period of student academic failure.

DISCUSSION QUESTIONS

1. What is classroom advocacy and why is it important?
2. What issues have you encountered that could benefit from classroom advocacy?
3. Why are evidence-based practices important for students with disabilities?
4. How do you advocate for students in your classroom and/or on your caseload?
5. Explain potential differences in classroom advocacy between a special education teacher who pushes in to general education classrooms and one who teaches in a self-contained classroom?

REFERENCES

Athanases, S. Z., & De Oliveira, L. C. (2008). Advocacy for equity in classrooms and beyond: New teachers' challenges and responses. *Teachers College Record, 110*(1), 64–104. https://doi.org/10.1177/016146810811000101

Americans with Disabilities Act of 1990, 42 U.S.C. § 12101.

Berlinghoff, D., & McLaughlin, V. L. (2022). *Practice-based standards for the preparation of special educators.* Council for Exceptional Children.

CAST. (2022). *The UDL guidelines.* https://udlguidelines.cast.org/

Council for Exceptional Children. (2020). *K12 initial standards and components.* https://exceptionalchildren.org/sites/default/files/2021-03/K12%20Initial%20 Standards%20and%20Components.pdf

Endrew F. v. Douglas County School District, 137 S. Ct. 988 (2017).

Every Student Succeeds Act of 2015, Pub. L. No. 114-95, § 4104.

Francis, G. L., Haines, J. S., & Nagro, S. A. (2017). Developing relationships with immigrant families: Learning by asking the right questions. *Teaching Exceptional Children, 50*(2), 95–105. https://doi.org/10.1177/0040059917720778

Goodwin, B. (2021). Zombie ideas in education. *Educational Leadership*, *78*(8), 44–49. https://www.ascd.org/el/articles/zombie-ideas-in-education

Individuals with Disabilities Education Act of 2004, 20 U.S.C. § 1400.

IRIS Center. (2014). *Evidence-based practices (part 1): Identifying and selecting a practice or program.* https://iris.peabody.vanderbilt.edu/module/ebp_01/

Kauffman, J. M., Anastasiou, D., Felder, M., Hornby, G., & Lopes, J. (2022). Recent debates in special and inclusive education. In R. Tierney, F. Rizvi, K. Ercikan, G. Smith, & R. Slee (Eds.), *International encyclopedia of education* (4th ed.). Elsevier.

Kauffman, J. M., Burke, M. D., & Anastasiou, D. (2022). Hard LRE choices in the era of inclusion: Rights and their implications. *Journal of Disability Policy Studies*. https://doi.org/10.1177/10442073221113074

Khazan, O. (2018, April 11). The myth of 'learning styles.' *The Atlantic.* https://www .theatlantic.com/science/archive/2018/04/the-myth-of-learning-styles/557687/

Markelz, A. M., & Bateman, D. F. (2022). *The essentials of special education law*. Rowman & Littlefield. https://rowman.com/ISBN/9781538150023/The -Essentials-of-Special-Education-Law

Nagro, S. A., Fraser, D. W., & Hooks, S. (2019). Lesson planning with engagement in mind: Proactive classroom management strategies for curriculum instruction. *Intervention in School and Clinic*, *54*(3), 131–140. https://doi.org/ 10.1177/1053451218767905

National Center for Learning Disabilities. (2018, March). *Agents of their own success: Self-advocacy skills and self-determination for students with disabilities in the era of personalized learning.* https://www.ncld.org/wp-content/uploads/2018/03/ Agents-of-Their-Own-Success_Final.pdf

Nelson, G., Cook, S. C., Zarate, K., Powell, S. R., Maggin, D. M., Drake, K. R., Kiss, A. J., Ford, J. W., Sun, L., & Espinas, D. R. (2022). A systematic review of meta-analyses in special education: Exploring the evidence base for high-leverage practices. *Remedial & Special Education*, *43*(5), 344–358. https://doi.org/ 10.1177/07419325211063491

Rozalski, M., Yell, M. L., & Warner, J. (2021). Free appropriate public education, the US Supreme Court, and developing and implementing individualized education programs. *Laws*, *10*(2), 38–49. https://doi.org/10.3390/laws10020038

Slee, R. (2018). *Inclusive education isn't dead, it just smells funny*. Routledge.

Taylor, S. J. (2016). Still caught in the continuum: A critical analysis of least restrictive environment and its effect on placement of students with intellectual disability. *Inclusion*, *4*(2), 56–74. https://doi.org/10.1352/2326-6988-4.2.56

Whitby, P., Marx, T., McIntire, J., & Wienke, W. (2013). Advocating for students with disabilities at the school level: Yips for special educators. *Teaching Exceptional Children*, *45*(5), 32–39. https://doi.org/10.1177/004005991304500504

Yell, M. L., & Prince, A. T. (2022). Why the continuum of alternative placements is essential. In Kauffman, J. M. (Ed.), *Revitalizing special education* (pp. 59–78). Emerald Publishing Limited. https://doi.org/10.1108/978-1-80117-494-720221003

Chapter Five

Ring of School Advocacy

The rings of advocacy are building outward, and the third ring of influence is school advocacy. School advocacy is where one seeks to find solutions at the school or district level rather than at the individual classroom level, as was discussed in the previous chapter. Each school, even within a larger district system, has its own context shaped in part by location, the student and family body served, cultural norms, existing resources, and institutional history. Special education teachers navigate these contextual factors on a daily basis to seek support for their students, and sometimes there is a need to change the context with which the school operates through advocacy. For example, special education teachers may recognize unique needs of students with disabilities that could be solved more universally than individually. They may want to advocate to make a school-level change to policies or procedures. School advocacy may involve advocating to build leadership or may require seeking solutions from outside stakeholders such as school board members or even district-level leaders. In chapter 5, we will explore the school advocacy ring (figure 5.1) and answer these essential questions:

1. What is the school advocacy ring and why is it important?
2. What are some current opportunities for school advocacy?
3. How do you advocate for students in your school?
4. Where can I find more information on school advocacy?

Figure 5.1.   The School Advocacy Ring

WHAT IS THE SCHOOL ADVOCACY RING
AND WHY IS IT IMPORTANT?

Each school has a culture all its own. In addition to being a safe place for learning, schools are healthcare facilities, nutritional centers, opportunities for professional development, community hubs, and more. In any given school, dozens of faculty and staff members come to school each day to ensure students and staff have a clean and safe place to learn and work, maintain student records, provide services, participate in meetings, prepare and serve meals, provide community services, create a network of family and community supports, and of course, teach children. This **nested system**, or a system with multiple elements enclosing one another, is complex and dynamic despite having regular routines and schedules. Within this nested system, special education teachers are well situated to understand what is working well within their school contexts and what is not. Special educators interact with many of the ranging professionals across the nested system to ensure their students' needs are being met in both academic and nonacademic settings every day during school hours. When things are working smoothly, all faculty and staff work together to ensure that students are receiving their free appropriate public education (FAPE). When any one portion of a nested system is lacking, the ripple effects are felt more broadly. In these instances, school advocacy is needed to help improve one or more aspects of school operations, school culture, working conditions, or learning environments.

There are a range of instances when advocating for policy changes school-wide can be beneficial to the student body as part of the nested system. Consider for a moment a school where students in a **life skills classroom** are included with their nondisabled peers during music and art. Due to a new school policy, aimed at reducing problematic student behaviors in the hallways, the art and music teachers now travel to individual classrooms rather than students walking to the art or music rooms. The special education students also have to travel to their nondisabled peers' classroom to receive art and music in an inclusive setting. However, there are no desks for these students joining the general education classrooms, so they have to sit at the computer station, at a small group reading table, or on the ground in the classroom library. The special education teacher realizes her students are unable to fully participate in art or music because they are still physically excluded from the lesson. In fact, since the policy change, this teacher gets weekly reports that her students have been asked to leave class due to disruptive behaviors. The assistant principal mentions the strain this is causing on office staff who have to sit with these students in the main office. The art teacher says she would rather these students have alternate assignments because they cannot use paint near the classroom computers. Finally, the special educator decides to give up her planning period on art and music days to push in and try to support student engagement in an already overcrowded learning space.

There are clear ripple effects of a school policy within a nested system affecting students, teachers, staff, and school building leaders. The previous scenario is an example of a well-intentioned school policy with negative **unintended consequences**. Unintended consequences, or unforeseen outcomes at the time of decision-making, create new opportunities for advocacy. In this example, the special education teacher can appreciate the shift in school policy since hallway and bathroom safety have been discussed at recent school board meetings, but she also understands her students cannot engage in inclusive education if there is no space created for such learning to occur. Situations like this require a school-wide change, which may unfortunately be overlooked without the vital perspective of special educators.

WHAT ARE SOME CURRENT OPPORTUNITIES FOR SCHOOL ADVOCACY?

Unlike classroom advocacy issues where individual or small groups of students are affected, school advocacy opportunities are about school policies that affect many students. Oftentimes, these policies are not solely the decision of one person; rather, they are the result of various stakeholders making determinations based on a variety of factors. Below are a few opportunities that may require school advocacy.

Related Services

Students with disabilities are required to receive special education services and related services to receive FAPE in the least restrictive environment (LRE). Related services are provided for a student to benefit from special education services. According to the Individuals with Disabilities Education Act (IDEA, 2004):

> Related services means transportation and such developmental, corrective, and other supportive services as are required to assist a child with a disability to benefit from special education, and includes speech-language pathology and audiology services, interpreting services, psychological services, physical and occupational therapy, recreation, including therapeutic recreation, early identification and assessment of disabilities in children, counseling services, including rehabilitation counseling, orientation and mobility services, and medical services for diagnostic or evaluation purposes. Related services also include school health services and school nurse services, social work services in schools, and parent counseling and training.

There are many services that may qualify under the related services provision of IDEA. It is important to remember that related services are to help a student have greater access to and benefit from special education services.

Busing Procedures

One important related service for some students with disabilities is transportation. If a student cannot physically access a school due to a lack of transportation, then clearly the student is not receiving FAPE. Transportation can include travel to and from school and between schools; travel in and around school buildings; and specialized equipment such as special or adapted buses, lifts, and ramps. A student's individualized education program (IEP) team is responsible for determining if transportation is required and how the transportation services should be implemented. If a student requires transportation, consider the implications of transportation for that student. Some questions to consider follow:

1. Does the bus drop off and pick up from school at the same time as other students? If not, does having different times separate students with disabilities from arrival and dismissal procedures for students without disabilities?

2. Does riding the special education bus create a stigma and contribute to an exclusionary culture among students and staff?
3. Are accommodating buses provided for field trips for students with and without disabilities?

Adapted buses are necessary for students with adaptive needs, and they are essential in providing FAPE. Yet it is important to think about school busing procedures and whether any unintended consequences are occurring. Advocating for change may involve challenging issues such as transportation budgets, limited number of buses, and availability of drivers, but also school/district policy makers may have only considered these types of issues and have not considered the effects of busing procedures on students. As a special education teacher who keeps students at the forefront of policy making, perhaps your advocacy is needed.

Pull-Out Scheduling

Other common related services include speech therapy, occupational therapy, physical therapy, and counseling. Since there are only so many minutes in a school day, oftentimes **pull-out scheduling** is used where students are pulled out of their regular class schedule to receive a related service. Some schools tend to provide related services during classes that are considered "less essential," such as art, music, and physical education—in other words, the nonacademic classes. Unfortunately for these students, missing extracurricular activities can have negative effects on academics, engagement, and overall school enjoyment (Furda & Shuleski, 2019). It is likely that the related service provider has a large caseload of students that encompasses multiple schools. Therefore, scheduling conflicts are bound to occur. But consider the ramifications of **blanket policies** that mandate when and where a related service must take place.

Individualization is a central tenet to any student's IEP (Markelz & Bateman, 2022). Blanket school policies may come in conflict with this principle. When developing a student's IEP and discussing related services, the IEP team should consider the students' likes, dislikes, and school subject preferences. Take for example a student with speech services who is particularly excited about art. The student's class is scheduled to have art during last period, but that is when the speech pathologist is in the building working with students. Rather than the student missing art class to receive her speech therapy, finding an accommodation to allow that student to participate in an art class seems important. What if other classmates also receive speech therapy and are forced to miss art class? Perhaps a schedule change is necessary to accommodate the entire class. Although this is one specific example, depending on school contexts, there are many opportunities to advocate for related service policies.

Placement Predetermination

The discussion around full inclusion versus a continuum of LRE placements was introduced in chapter 4 and will be expanded in chapter 8. Schools, however, sometimes adopt LRE policies where all students with disabilities are taught in the general education classroom (e.g., co-teaching model). Or students with mild disabilities (e.g., specific learning disabilities, other health impairments) are only taught with co-teaching models, while students with more severe disabilities are educated in self-contained classrooms. Although there are documented benefits to inclusive practices (Wehmeyer et al., 2021), as previously mentioned, blanket policies about where students with certain types of disabilities are placed oppose the individualization of IEP decision-making.

The US Supreme Court has not ruled on a case concerning LRE; however, four prominent US Circuit Court cases have established controlling and persuasive authority across the country. The four cases are *Roncker v. Walter* (1983), *Daniel R. R. v. State Board of Education* (1989), *DeVries v. Fairfax County School Board* (1989), and *Sacramento City Unified School District Board of Education v. Rachel H.* (1994). According to Markelz and Bateman (2022), common factors among LRE case law have established the following:

1. The general education classroom is the preferred educational setting.
2. Educational benefit (i.e., FAPE) supersedes social benefit regarding placement in the general education classroom.
3. School personnel have professional expertise to make placement decisions.
4. School personnel may consider the effects of placement on the student's teachers and peers.
5. If a more restrictive environment than the general education classroom is warranted, the students should be integrated with their peers to the maximum extent appropriate.

Case law is clear that **predetermination** of a student's placement is a violation of IDEA (Yell, 2019). Furthermore, placement decisions based on factors other than a student's educational needs such as disability category, availability of services, or administrative convenience are not valid reasons. Only through a comprehensive evaluation process and IEP development can a student's needs and goals be identified. Then, special education services can be determined. LRE placement decisions must follow this process and examine along the continuum the most appropriate placement for the student to receive FAPE.

Discipline Policies

Schools are meant to be safe and supportive environments that are conducive to teaching and learning. Although school administrators often complain that students with disabilities are immune from discipline because of protections under IDEA (Osborne & Russo, 2009), this is not true. All students are expected to follow school rules to maintain conducive learning environments. Students with disabilities are, however, guaranteed FAPE under IDEA, which provides them additional procedural safeguards.

One important safeguard for students with disabilities is the right to be protected from discrimination based on their disability. Just like students with a reading disability would not be disciplined for reading below grade level, students with an emotional disturbance should not be disciplined for demonstrating behaviors associated with their disability. Schools must be proactive when addressing problem behaviors related to students' disability. Procedures should be taken such as conducting a **manifestation determination** to understand whether a problem behavior is related to students' disability. **Functional behavioral assessments** can be conducted to identify what is causing a problem behavior. And **behavior intervention plans** should be developed along with behavior goals within the IEP to teach and reinforce appropriate behaviors.

When schools and/or districts adopt discipline policies (e.g., "three strikes and you're out") that do not examine the nuance behind behavioral actions, nor proactively reinforce appropriate behaviors, there is the potential for violating procedural safeguards. Students with disabilities can be disciplined with time-outs, detentions, point/grade reductions, conference calls home, and short-term suspensions. Exclusively relying on **punishment procedures**, however, does not foster a positive school culture. Given special education teachers' training in classroom management and positive behavior strategies, advocating for systems like school-wide positive behavioral interventions and support (SW-PBIS) can significantly affect the school environment in positive ways (Bradshaw et al., 2008).

A second procedural safeguard concerning the discipline of students with disabilities protects them from unfair or mistaken long-term suspensions. In 1975, case law set by *Goss v. Lopez* determined that removal from school of 10 days or less constitutes a short-term suspension. Suspensions over 10 days are considered long-term suspensions. For students with disabilities, cumulative or consecutive suspensions over 10 days are considered a **change in placement**. Change of placements can only be determined by the IEP team—which includes the student (if age appropriate) and the student's legal guardians. Therefore, if a school is wanting to suspend or expel a student with a disability for more than 10 days, the IEP team must first meet to consider how the student's special education services will continue while they are in their new placement. Even if the suspension is for one day over the 10-day cutoff, the student is entitled to FAPE in their new placement for that day.

In general, school-wide discipline policies that exclusively focus on punishing inappropriate behaviors and resort to suspensions may become legally indefensible concerning students with disabilities. Without positive reinforcement procedures that are proactive in encouraging supportive learning environments, students with disabilities may be repeatedly removed from the learning environment and subsequently denied FAPE. Special education teachers should be aware that students with disabilities too often face harsh and exclusionary disciplinary action at schools (US Department of Education, 2022). Therefore, advocacy for school-wide proactive discipline policies will not only benefit students with disabilities but will foster a positive school culture for all students and staff.

Adapted Physical Education

Within IDEA (2004) is language that provides students with disabilities access to physical education (PE). Specially designed instruction may be needed to meet students' individual needs even if that means providing something different than the general PE curriculum (McNamara et al., 2021). Adaptions to PE can include changes to the equipment, boundaries or playing field, time, rules, or specific actions. According to IDEA, adapted PE should reflect general PE curriculum to the greatest extent possible, allowing students with ranging needs to access health and recreation. Physical education has several documented benefits for students with disabilities including opportunities to socialize with nondisabled peers, improved fitness, and increased on-task behaviors (Wong et al., 2015). Adapting PE to be accessible to more students is a logical aim; however, only about 13% of students with disabilities receive adapted PE (Centers for Disease Control and Prevention, 2015).

There are many bureaucratic and logistical barriers preventing students with disabilities access to adaptive PE (McNamara et al., 2021). For example, adapted PE teachers are not typically staffed at every school. This means that one adaptive PE teacher may have upward of 100 students on their caseload within an entire district (Trad et al., 2021). Furthermore, general and adapted physical educators are often not invited to IEP meetings and do not have opportunities to be part of the IEP team. Therefore, insight and feedback about adaptive PE goals during the IEP development stage are missing (McNamara et al., 2021). Awareness and involvement are key to this issue. Assuring school-level awareness of what is expected under IDEA (2004) for students with disabilities struggling to access PE and involvement of PE teachers in the IEP process are great first steps.

HOW DO YOU ADVOCATE FOR STUDENTS IN YOUR SCHOOL?

Regardless of the school, keys to successful school advocacy are maintaining trusted relationships when seeking stakeholder input and prioritizing data-based decision-making to inform systems and operations with an openness for professional learning (Weber et al., 2022). School advocacy can be tricky given the nested nature of schools. But once special educators understand whom to advocate to and what to advocate for, things begin to make more sense. Connecting student needs with **change agents** in the school such as the school principal or special education chair can help shed light on whom to advocate to. In some situations, there may be more than one stakeholder involved in changing a school policy or procedure. Advocacy could require partnering with multiple groups to improve student experiences. Figure 5.2 illustrates a typical organizational and leadership structure for a school and its district. Like the self and classroom advocacy rings, advocating at the school level is a process. The next section will cover how to advocate for your school.

Identify and Understand the Problem

The process of advocating for your school relies on having a comprehensive understanding of the needs and issues surrounding your school. Many of us want to make changes when we see problems or injustices, and we support that desire. However, it is *very* important to have a good understanding of what is happening and more importantly, why something is happening. There may be specific reasons why existing policies are in place, or there may be organizational barriers preventing a change that require a broader understanding of the nested system. While listening, learn about how the process of concern affects others and which parties are involved, understand the history of the issue, and realize others may have tried to make changes previously. If these efforts have failed, try to understand the reasons that these changes were

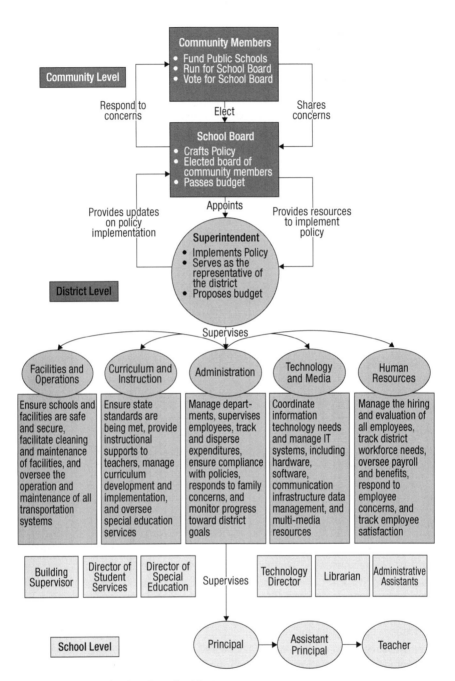

Figure 5.2. Organizational Leadership Structure

not enacted and where advocacy efforts may have fallen short. In listening and learning, viable solutions may present themselves. Gathering multiple perspectives will help when trying to think through potential unintended consequences that might undermine your progress in enacting change.

To highlight the importance of understanding a problem, consider this example. A new teacher noticed that there was often trash and debris scattered across the local elementary school playground. Not only was the trash unsightly, but it made it difficult for her students to enjoy the playground and have a safe experience. The teacher assumed a lazy custodian was responsible for not cleaning up the playground. Before approaching the principal to complain about the problem, the teacher started talking to others. She first learned that the custodial staff hours had been significantly reduced related to a combination of budget cuts and a lack of applicants for the part-time position. She also learned that there had been major cuts to the city's budget related to trash removal. Local residents did not have a place to put their trash nor have it removed on a consistent basis. What the teacher originally thought was a lazy custodian turned out to be a larger problem with more complex issues at play. Sometimes an initial thought about how to solve the problem is not always the right way. As the teacher in this scenario learned, understanding the complexities of an issue is critical to successful advocacy at the school level where the nested system is often composed of nuanced interactions.

Invite Stakeholders

One way to gather multiple perspectives and understanding of these complex problems is to invite stakeholders to join in partnership to seek a common solution. Learning from others can shed light on where there is **convergence** around an issue and where groups differ. Identifying points of convergence can help clarify a viable pathway forward, thus directing advocacy efforts. Does the administrator see this issue as a priority? Are their parents pushing a similar agenda/issue? Are there school board members who have an agenda that may be supportive to the specific area of need? Are there other politicians who also have a similar agenda? Think about why they have these thoughts or beliefs and where there is potential convergence. Gathering this information will help determine if change is possible. If multiple stakeholders find convergence, momentum for change starts to grow.

To identify areas of convergence, take others' viewpoints. This means trying to understand their **organizing principles**, or the lens through which others make sense of an issue. There is debate among social science researchers about how much influence organizing principles have on one's agency—that is, factors in society that control choice making such as race, gender, religion, and social class (Gibbs, 2017). Organizing principles can be shaped by personal experiences, beliefs, priorities, and associations. For example, people who view themselves as being members of a marginalized group may prioritize the needs of this subgroup and explore an issue as it specifically relates to their association with this subgroup. Other stakeholders may view the same issue quite differently because they organize their thinking around their religious beliefs and consider how this issue affects their ability to practice in their religion. Still other stakeholders may come to the same issue differently by organizing their thinking around a particular social movement or being focused on job security or traditional family values. Learning about others' organizing principles will help clarify where common ground can be established.

Determine Solutions

Whether in a classroom co-teaching, eating lunch with colleagues, attending school leadership meetings, or even talking with friends and family outside of school, each interaction provides an opportunity to influence others. Systemic school-level change can sprout from these individual interactions, such as changes to better working conditions, changes to help you do your job. Even more broadly, individual interactions can spark systemic school-level changes to support the profession of special education that have transformed the lives of children with disabilities.

Despite the ripple effect that change can have as it moves across a nested system, keep the focus on students when determining solutions. Teachers, by nature are working with the intention that it is their job to improve the lives of the students they serve. Within this context, decide what success looks like and maximize flexibility in the definition of a solution to achieve this success. It is no secret teachers need better working conditions (and respect) because teachers are leaving the profession faster than new teachers can be prepared (Billingsley & Bettini, 2019). With this in mind, the best way to get others to buy in to any change is to keep the focus on what is necessary for improving educational conditions of students. Rising tides lift all boats, so the saying goes. If special educators are able to (a) understand their role within the nested system including how they interact with other stakeholders in the organizational structure, (b) recognize their organizing principles and the implications of how they make sense of the issues, (c) invite those with differing perspectives to partner in solutions, and (d) maximize convergence, viable solutions will become apparent.

WHERE CAN I FIND MORE INFORMATION ON SCHOOL ADVOCACY?

Advocating for School-Wide Positive Behavioral Interventions and Supports

 This website from the Center on Positive Behavioral Interventions & Supports (PBIS) explains the foundational elements of PBIS and outlines the three distinct tiers. Within the website, you can also find tools, publications, presentations, and videos all about PBIS. Start exploring at https://www.pbis.org/topics/school-wide.

Lecture on Placement Decisions by Dr. Mitchell Yell

 In this YouTube video published by the IEP Technical Assistance Center, Dr. Yell, a respected scholar in the field of special education law, delivers a lecture on advocacy strategies regarding placement decisions, least restrictive environment, and the continuum of placements. You can watch this informative lecture at https://www.youtube.com/watch?v=VZ2RYi2zNDQ.

Positive, Proactive Approaches to Supporting Children with Disabilities

 Regulatory guidance from the US Department of Education provides a description of effective practices to support students with disabilities. This policy support document mentions topics such as preventing exclusionary discipline, universal academic and behavioral supports, targeted and intensive supports, and culturally and linguistically responsive practices. Read it at https://sites.ed.gov/idea/files/guide-positive-proactive-approaches-to-supporting-children-with-disabilities.pdf.

School Discipline for Students with Disabilities

 Understood.com explains the procedural safeguards afforded to students with disabilities with regard to discipline. Topics addressed include changes in placement, manifestation determinations, functional behavioral assessments (FBAs), and behavior intervention plans (BIPs). Visit https://www.understood.org/en/articles/school-discipline-the-rights-of-students-with-ieps-and-504-plans.

KEY TERMS

behavior intervention plan: A written plan that focuses on teaching and reinforcing appropriate student behaviors.

blanket policy: Proposed action that acts similarly to a variety of factors regardless of the effect due to individual circumstances.

change agent: An individual with the knowledge and skills to effect change within an organization.

change in placement: A change to the IEP that substantially affects the composition of the educational program and services provided to the student.

convergence: The act of moving toward union or unity.

functional behavioral assessment: A process to identify what is causing students' challenging behaviors.

life skills classroom: An instructional setting that is self-contained, typically reserved for students with more intense academic and functional needs.

manifestation determination: A process to understand whether a problem behavior is related to the student's disability.

nested system: An organization with multiple elements that affect one another.

organizing principle: Core assumption or central reference point from which everything else is evaluated.

predetermination: When the IEP or a component of the IEP is finalized prior to the IEP meeting.

pull-out scheduling: When special education teachers remove students on their caseload to provide services in a setting separate from the general education classroom.

punishment procedures: Consequences that focus on decreasing inappropriate student behaviors.

unintended consequences: Unforeseen outcomes at the time of decision-making.

DISCUSSION QUESTIONS

1. How do organizing principles affect a person's perspective on an issue?
2. What is the school advocacy ring and why is it important?
3. Describe the contextual factors that influence your school's nested system.
4. What are some barriers to advocating at the school level?
5. What are some current school advocacy opportunities in your school?

REFERENCES

Billingsley, B., & Bettini, E. (2019). Special education teacher attrition and retention: A review of the literature. *Review of Educational Research*, *89*(5), 697–744. https://doi.org/10.3102/0034654319862495

Bradshaw, C. P., Koth, C. W., Bevans, K. B., Ialongo, N., & Leaf, P. J. (2008). The impact of school-wide positive behavioral interventions and supports (PBIS) on the organizational health of elementary schools. *School Psychology Quarterly*, *23*(4), 462–473. https://psycnet.apa.org/doi/10.1037/a0012883

Centers for Disease Control and Prevention. (2015). *Results from the school health policies and practices study 2014*. http://www.cdc.gov/healthyyouth/data/shpps/pdf/shpps-508-final_101315.pdf

Daniel R. R. v. State Board of Education, 874 F.2d 1036 (5th Cir. 1989).

DeVries v. Fairfax County School Board, 853 F.2d 264 (4th Cir. 1989).

Furda, M., & Shuleski, M. (2019). The impact of extracurriculars on academic performance and school perception. *Excellence in Education Journal*, *8*(1), 64–90. https://eric.ed.gov/?id=EJ1208711

Gibbs, B. J. (2017, August 21). Structuration theory. *Encyclopedia Britannica*. https://www.britannica.com/topic/structuration-theory

Goss v. Lopez, 419 U.S. 565 (1975).

Individuals with Disabilities Education Act of 2004, 20 U.S.C. § 1400.

Markelz, A. M., & Bateman, D. F. (2022). *The essentials of special education law*. Rowman & Littlefield.

McNamara, S. W. T., Lieberman, L., Weiner, B., & McMullen, B. (2021). Discussing adapted physical education during IEP meetings: First-hand parent experiences and a supporting tool. *Journal of Research in Special Educational Needs*, *21*(4), 302–311. https://doi.org/10.1111/1471-3802.12528

Osborne, A. G., & Russo, C. J. (2009). *Discipline in special education.* Corwin Press.

Roncker v. Walter, 700 F.2d 1058 (6th Cir. 1983).

Sacramento City Unified School District Board of Education v. Rachel H., 14 F.3d 1398 (9th Cir. 1994).

Trad, A. M., Richards, K. A. R., & Wilson, W. J. (2021). Strategies to increase self-, student, and discipline advocacy in adapted physical education. *TEACHING Exceptional Children*, *54*(1), 52–62. https://doi.org/10.1177/00400599211018838

US Department of Education. (2022, July 19). *New guidance helps schools support students with disabilities and avoid discriminatory use of discipline*. https://www.ed.gov/news/press-releases/new-guidance-helps-schools-support-students-disabilities-and-avoid-discriminatory-use-discipline

Weber, M., Freeman, M., Justina, Y., Diaz, Y. Y., Stephanie, M., & Aigner, A. (2022). *Advocating for youth experiencing trauma*. National Association of School Psychologists.

Wehmeyer, M. L., Shogren, K. A., & Kurth, J. (2021). The state of inclusion with students with intellectual and developmental disabilities in the United States. *Journal of Policy and Practice in Intellectual Disabilities*, *18*(1), 36–43. https://doi.org/10.1111/jppi.12332

Wong, C., Odom, S. L., Hume, K. A., Cox, A. W., Fettig, A., Kucharczyk, S., & Schultz, T. R. (2015). Evidence-based practices for children, youth, and young adults with autism spectrum disorder: A comprehensive review. *Journal of Autism and Developmental Disorders*, *45*(7), 1951–1966.

Yell, M. L. (2019). *The law and special education* (5th ed.). Pearson Education.

Chapter Six

Ring of State Advocacy

Special education teachers are well positioned to recognize problems and understand realistic solutions that can be addressed at the state level. No one has better firsthand knowledge of the consequences of state policies after implementation than teachers. Whether intentional or not, state policies reverberate across school contexts and can positively or negatively affect students with disabilities and their teachers. The fourth ring of influence is state advocacy, and it relates to leading change in state-level education policy and implementation guidelines. Through state advocacy, special education teachers advocate to their state-level elected representatives and department of education personnel. As the rings of advocacy continue to expand, the types of issues that require advocacy also broaden. State-level change must be applicable across all school contexts. Although issues at the state level may become entwined in bureaucratic procedures, policy makers recognize that students matter. Educating the next generation matters. And a teacher's voice matters when advocating to affect state policy makers' actions. In this chapter, we will explore the state advocacy ring (figure 6.1) and answer these essential questions:

1. What is the state advocacy ring and why is it important?
2. What are some current opportunities for state advocacy?
3. How do you advocate at the state level?
4. Where can I find more information on state-level advocacy?

Figure 6.1. The State Advocacy Ring

WHAT IS THE STATE ADVOCACY RING
AND WHY IS IT IMPORTANT?

Each state's government is modeled after the federal government, which consists of the executive, legislative, and judicial branches. When it comes to education, state governments have a great deal of flexibility and autonomy (Nagro et al., 2022). Each state has its own department of education where federal- and state-level policies are translated into plans for implementation and **oversight**. For example, the Individuals with Disabilities Education Act (IDEA, 2004), passed at the federal level, spells out what states must do to meet the needs of students with disabilities. The states interpret these rules to then pass their own laws on how to apply the rules of IDEA within their state. The federal government creates incentives, aid, and grant programs to encourage state governments to align their priorities with those of the federal government. This is one of the reasons state advocacy is so important.

States typically have to publish a plan for enacting federal policy to become eligible for the various forms of federal funding. For example, on March 11, 2021, the American Rescue Plan Act of 2021 was signed into law. Almost $3 billion of the $130 billion allocated to the US Department of Education was **earmarked** for IDEA grant awards for the 2021 fiscal year. Each state submitted its plans in which COVID-19 pandemic–related needs and requested supplemental funds were outlined. Funds were then given to state educational agencies to safely reopen and sustain schools after the effect of the pandemic. Through advocacy, state government officials can learn about the value added through special education as well as existing areas of need so that special education is front and center when state leaders write plans such as those submitted for the American Rescue Plan Act of 2021 funds. When these same state officials make plans for how to use the funds provided by the federal government through a process called **appropriation**, it always helps to have informed voices advocating for those funds to be directed toward addressing the needs of students with disabilities.

As a special educator, you are an informed voice. **Hot button** issues playing out in schools such as current societal trends, political agendas, or curriculum shifts often draw public attention. Such attention brings both scrutiny and support. Special education teachers have a unique purview as to how the infiltration of contemporary issues into schools through state-led initiatives affects student learning and child development. Therefore, the voice of special educators through state advocacy is extremely important for maintaining a student-centered mindset when policy changes are occurring, as opposed to getting swept up in temporary topics used for political gain.

WHAT ARE SOME CURRENT OPPORTUNITIES FOR STATE ADVOCACY?

In this section, you will learn about current opportunities to advocate for at the state level. Even though the rights of students with disabilities and the special education field have made tremendous progress over the past several decades, there are opportunities for betterment. Special educators should never assume the field has reached its **pinnacle** or that access, inclusion, and equity for students will be maintained without effort. There is still much work to do and issues to advocate for.

Teacher Licensure

Education is not mentioned in the US Constitution; however, the 10th Amendment states, "The powers not delegated to the United States by the Constitution, nor prohibited by it to the States, are reserved to the States respectively, or to the people." Therefore, education is a matter determined by individual states. Even though there are federal statutes that provide monetary incentives to align state policies with federal priorities, states have the right to adopt or reject those incentives (Markelz & Bateman, 2022). Rarely do states pass up federal dollars, though, and today the federal government and state education policies such as IDEA and the Every Student Succeeds Act

(ESSA, 2015) are intertwined. Given the individuality of states to regulate education, there is expected variation in state policy implementation guidance. One area that special education teachers should be aware of is teacher licensure requirements.

When ESSA was passed in 2015 (as the reauthorization of No Child Left Behind [NCLB, 2001]), there were edits to the language around teacher qualifications. Because IDEA (2004) had language about "highly qualified" taken from NCLB, the edits in ESSA meant the language in IDEA was also edited. The term *highly qualified* was removed from the statute, and now the requirement to be a special education teacher, as described by ESSA (2015) is as follows:

1. Each person employed as a special education teacher in the State who teaches elementary school, middle school, or secondary school must have obtained full State certification as a special education teacher (including participating in an alternate route to certification as a special educator, if such alternate route meets minimum requirements);
2. Has not had special education certification or licensure requirements waived on an emergency, temporary, or provisional basis; and
3. Holds at least a bachelor's degree.

The areas within these requirements that allow for greatest state flexibility are **alternative route programs** and licensure requirement waivers for emergency, temporary, or provisional teachers. Chapter 9 will explore the issue of persistent special education teacher shortages in greater detail, but states are facing a crisis concerning the lack of special educators (Peyton et al., 2021). The teacher shortage is not a new problem; rather, it has been developing for decades (Sutcher et al., 2019). Federal and state policy decisions in the 1990s gained momentum for alternative routes to licensure that often "fast-tracked" personnel into hard-to-fill positions. Unfortunately for students and the profession, lowering the bar to entry only exacerbated the problem and has led the field to its current shortage crisis (Brownell & Leko, 2018). It should be noted that not all alternative routes to special education preparation lack quality, rigor, and comprehensiveness (Rosenberg et al., 2007). Alternative routes that lack the intensity of **traditional preparation programs**, however, often produce teachers of lesser quality and profession readiness (Leko et al., 2012).

Even though minimum qualifications for becoming a special education teacher have been established by federal statutes, states maintain substantial authority on what "state certification" means or how rigorous alternative route programs must be. In addition, states can use funding to attract applicants into preparation programs through scholarships, grants, and other monetary incentives. Teacher preparation research clearly indicates that well-prepared teachers stay in the profession longer and have a more positive effect on student outcomes (Brownell et al., 2010). Advocating at the state level for high standards in special education teacher licensure is, therefore, a paramount issue.

Reading Wars

There is a decades-long debate that is still very energized about the best way to help students learn how to read. Historically, this debate was between **phonics** and **whole language** approaches. Whole language instruction is based on the philosophy that students will learn to read naturally, in context, if exposed to many high-interest books. Phonics advocates, however, explain that not all students naturally pick up literacy skills (Barshay, 2020). Explicit phonics instruction is needed, therefore, for all students to learn to read. In the mid-1990s, the term **balanced literacy** was popularized to merge the promising elements of both phonics and whole language (Fisher et al., 2023). The debate was not settled because critics pointed to the lack of systematic phonics instruction in balanced literacy and an overdependence on cueing, independent reading time, and leveled reading (Barshay, 2020). More recently, researchers have shifted the debate to a focus on the **science of reading**, but this term seems to have only reinforced tension within the field given the lack of consensus from reading researchers (e.g., Semingson & Kerns, 2021) and veteran teachers (e.g., Fisher et al., 2023) regarding the ideal approach to improving student literacy. Most recently, science of reading debates have also included recommendations to account for aspects that make strong readers in addition to learning decoding, phonics, and fluency such as the developmental stages of children (Fisher et al., 2023). It is not clear where the reading wars will go next, but what is clear is that students with disabilities are performing well below their nondisabled peers in literacy at all levels of education.

States invest significant portions of their education budgets annually to early literacy, research-based literacy curriculums, reading recovery efforts, and professional development opportunities so that schools and teachers can improve reading and writing outcomes for all students, including students with disabilities. In 2022, the average reading score for both fourth and eighth grade students decreased significantly compared to 2019 (US Department of Education, 2022). These significant declines were true for 30 states and jurisdictions when looking at the fourth-grade data, and while 18 states and jurisdictions stayed the same, there were no states with improved reading scores

(US Department of Education, 2022). More alarming is that students with disabilities are performing many standard deviations below their nondisabled peers on these same reading assessments. States will be seeking solutions to declining reading scores because these data suggest changes are needed to the current approach. Accessing your state-, district-, school-, and class-level reading data can help you to understand where your class sits contextually within these national data. Seize all opportunities to share your teaching experiences with those who will listen. This may include participating in research studies or engaging with statewide training and technical assistance centers such as to your state's CEEDAR Center (visit https://ceedar.education.ufl .edu/ to find out details about your state). Researchers want to hear from the field as to what is working. State departments of education will be looking to those researchers for guidance on the next best steps. State funding decisions tend to be supported by research findings. Involving yourself in research opportunities and partnerships will create opportunities for your voice to influence state curriculum decisions.

Hot-Button Issues

In loco parentis is a Latin phrase that means "in place of the parent." This **common law** principle has been ingrained in school authority since the early days of public education. In essence, in loco parentis is a transfer of rights from legal guardians to school personnel. Based on in loco parentis, principals and teachers have the authority to teach, guide, correct, and discipline students to accomplish educational objectives (Smith & Yell, 2013). Schools need autonomy and authority to work with students during the school day.

The line between how much autonomy and authority a school should have has been an ongoing debate that shifts with societal trends. Obviously, parents are hesitant to give schools absolute authority on what their child is taught or how their child is disciplined. Schools, however, need to have common curriculums and disciplinary procedures to maintain productive learning environments. Statutory, regulatory, and case laws have addressed a variety of hot-button topics over the years.

Corporal punishment was once a common form of discipline. The practice was deemed constitutional and not a violation of the "cruel and unusual punishment" clause of the Eighth Amendment to the US Constitution (*Ingraham v. Wright*, 1977). Thirty-one states, however, have statutorily banned corporal punishment in public schools (Gershoff & Font, 2016). The practice of corporal punishment has been in steady decline since the 1970s with less than 0.5% of schoolchildren receiving the disciplinary procedure today (Gershoff et al., 2015).

Separations between education and the right of religious freedom (per the First Amendment of the US Constitution) have continually been in conflict in public schools. Controversial topics such as prayer in school, teaching evolution, and sex education are still debated in courtrooms, state legislatures, and school board meetings. More recently, accurate representations of US history and race relations (e.g., critical race theory) have emerged as hotly debated topics concerning what should and should not be taught in public education (Borter, 2022).

As was discussed in chapter 5, all stakeholders will have organizing principles in which an issue is viewed. Furthermore, differing priorities will emerge when discussing complex topics. For example, one person may be approaching a topic with religious conviction, while another is seeking political opportunity. One person may have heard inaccurate information and is basing their opinion not on fact. Another person may be personally affected by an issue and is prioritizing their personal experience and not the experiences of others. There are countless organizing principles and priorities that people intentionally and unintentionally bring when discussing controversial topics. As special educators, professional expertise and direct experience working with students with disabilities is a rare yet powerful organizing principle. As state policy makers redraw the lines of in loco parentis, informing that debate and prioritizing what is best for students with disabilities is a needed voice.

Standardized Assessments

Access to public education for students with disabilities has evolved since the passage of the Education for All Handicapped Children Act of 1975 (now called IDEA). What was once defined as physical access to school buildings and classrooms, the term now encompasses access to challenging academic learning objectives based in the college- and career-ready general education curriculum (Nagro et al., 2022).

When NCLB (2001) was passed, the stated goal was to close academic achievement gaps by bringing every student up to state standards in reading and math. If states wanted to continue receiving federal funding through this legislative vehicle, they were required to monitor progress and demonstrate **adequate yearly progress**. Although flawed in many areas (Darling-Hammond, 2007), one positive development from NCLB was that students with disabilities were included as a subgroup on state assessment accountability measures. This meant schools were now responsible for the academic progress of students with disabilities. Rather than simply focusing on participation in general education classrooms, academic performance of this population was a priority. Schools could no longer ignore rigorous instruction for students with disabilities.

To measure academic performance across schools as a whole and various subgroups (e.g., race, ethnicity, socioeconomic status, English language learners, and disability), states developed standardized assessments. Just like students without disabilities, students with disabilities were required to take grade-level standardized assessments. To account for potential discrepancies between academic ability and grade-level performance, NCLB (2001) allowed a limited list of state-approved accommodations for students with individualized education programs (Markelz & Bateman, 2022). Individual states may have a variety of approved accommodations, but some common examples include braille or large-print exam books, extended time, distraction-free testing room, calculator, and screen-reading technology. Each state will have a list of approved standardized assessment accommodations.

The goals of NCLB (2001) to raise academic standards and bring all students to proficiency in reading and math were commendable. The rigid federal mandates and punitive measures, however, created an environment of "teaching to the test," and educational stakeholders realized reauthorization of the law was needed (Markelz & Bateman, 2022). The passage of ESSA (2015) maintained many of the positives of NCLB such as educational access, high standards, and school accountability. The legislation shifted authority away from the federal government and back to states and local districts. States are now more accountable in how they spend federal ESSA dollars and how their accountability systems are managed.

As special educators, knowing that state policy makers are more responsible for standardized assessments means your voice at the state level can make a difference. Measuring student performance is a good thing. At the same time, some students with disabilities are several grade levels behind their age-appropriate peers. Forcing these students to take grade-level assessments often results in resistance, embarrassment, failure, and a waste of time.

The ESSA (2015) does allow for students with more severe cognitive disabilities to take an alternative assessment based on achievement standards. This rule was initially established under NCLB (2001). A cap of 1% of students with disabilities, however, was set to prevent schools from hiding student data by disproportionately giving the alternative assessment to students who should be taking the state-administered assessment. Setting a percentage cap for how many students can take the alternative assessment seems justified. Subjectivity lies in whether 1% is the correct percentage. Debate about whether the 1% waiver should or should not be raised has and will continue to take place.

HOW DO YOU ADVOCATE AT THE STATE LEVEL?

Many advocacy groups or advocacy consultants direct their members to a specific model for advocacy. Table 6.1 illustrates the general approach. This five-step formulaic approach can be used when writing **policy briefs**, or short narratives, usually one or two pages, that include all five steps to introduce a topic, provide resources, and make a specific ask. The same steps can also be used when preparing talking points for congressional visits or writing letters to elected state officials. Along with these five steps, the following sections will summarize how to advocate in greater detail at the state level.

1. Open with a statement that engages your audience.
2. Present the problem.
3. Share a story or give an example of the problem.
4. Connect the issue to the audience's values, concerns, or self-interests.
5. Make your request (the "ask").

Identify and Understand the Problem

Before you present a problem to state-level stakeholders, it is important to clearly understand the problem. Many problems are complex and span several rings of advocacy. It is also important to identify the problem at hand, rather than getting caught up in symptoms of the problem. For example, it may seem logical to express concern about lag times for triannual evaluations during the school's faculty meeting when students' reevaluations are falling out of compliance. What seems like a school-level problem might be much larger and actually be taking place at the state level. To find out, state policy makers changed psychologists' licensure requirements. Psychologists are now required to renew their licenses every three years as opposed to every six years. Such a change had a ripple effect resulting in a significant increase in psychologists' retiring, and as a result, state shortages of school psychologists rose to an all-time high. The problem felt like a school issue since psychologists have been unable to complete triannual evaluations in a timely manner, but in reality, the problem is statewide. This is why understanding the problem before advocating for change is so important. Frontloading the time required to fully understand a problem can help set an advocacy plan on the right track. Fully understanding a problem requires an openness to learn. As layers are peeled back and the complexities of challenges become more evident, openness to change viewpoints can serve an advocate well. A well-informed advocate will have a more nuanced understanding of the problem and therefore, be likely to understand that issues are rarely as simple as they first appear.

Table 6.1. Advocacy Meeting Checklist

Process	Example	Tip
Open with a statement that engages your audience.	Hi, Delegate Smith, I remember meeting you when you had a town hall last year. I loved your speech, particularly how you expressed support for our schools. Thanks for taking the time to talk about this important issue!	If you've ever met with this person or have a mutual connection, now is the time to share!
Present the problem.	As you may know, state funding is running out for the after-school program in our district.	Keep this part short and to the point, but make sure to transition in a way that is not too jarring or abrasive.
Share a story or give an example of the problem.	I've spoken to so many community members who have benefited from this program. A woman in my book club was particularly upset to hear that the funding might be pulled. She said her kids absolutely adore their teachers and have made so many friends. While her child has been in the program, she has been able to pick up some extra hours at her job, which has helped her make ends meet. We are all heartbroken by the thought that these teachers might get laid off because they make such a difference.	Share personal anecdotes that are directly connected to the problem or issue. Find a way to link seemingly small, isolated challenges to more well-known or pressing issues.
Connect your issue to the audience's values, concerns, or self-interests.	I've recently heard you speak about the importance of supporting our schools, including our teachers, families, and, of course, students. I know this program has helped and will continue to help not just our students but our whole community. In fact, I have a letter signed by over 500 community members who support funding our after-school program.	Find a way to connect your ask to their agenda. If they are a policy maker, look up their priorities before the meeting. What committee do they sit on? It's always helpful to demonstrate that your issue has the attention of many concerned voters.
Make your request (the "ask").	That's why I'm asking that you consider supporting or cosponsoring the bill put forth by Delegate Lee. This bill will maintain funding for after-school programs throughout the district. It's such an important step to ensuring each child's needs are met. I sincerely appreciate your time and consideration!	Always come to a meeting with a solution—even if that solution accomplishes only one aspect of your broader goal. Always thank them for their time and consideration, and be sure to follow up with a thank-you message shortly after.

Invite Stakeholders

Sharing personal stories and connecting to stakeholder values are two great strategies for making solution-finding activities a group affair. The more that people feel the problem is "their'" problem, the more likely that momentum will grow for seeking solutions that everyone can agree on. This means figuring out ways to share your perspectives with others seeking solutions to similar problems, which may require working with folks in your school, district, or region to gain attention of state-level agencies. But where do you go to find state-level stakeholders? A great place to start seeking potential allies is by doing some research to understand where your elected officials stand on key issues. You can do so by checking elected officials' websites, media releases, and voting records to clarify where they stand on issues that matter to you. Additionally, seeking out state department education personnel who oversee initiatives, projects, or programs that directly relate to areas of interest can help with identifying stakeholders who will have vested interests in the issues that matter to you as well.

Determine Solutions

Given that state-level problems are often complex and nuanced, state-level advocacy solutions will require careful consideration of these nuances. Political scientist John Kingdon (2011) identified a three-streams model that can help with setting advocacy agendas and becoming more effective at enacting long-term systematic change (figure 6.2). Three streams to consider when advocating for change are the **problem stream**, **policy stream**, and **political stream**. The problem stream is established when a condition is interpreted in a way that requires attention, focus, and action. In other words, there is a defined problem that stakeholders feel the effects of and can understand its causes.

The policy stream is about whether a solution is available. Within the policy stream, lists of potential proposals for addressing the problem stream are created. After consideration, a narrowed list of viable pathways forward is agreed on. This short list of policy proposals is influenced by aspects such as feasibility, likelihood of gaining consensus, options for adoption, and anticipation of drawbacks. The problem and policy streams must be coupled to improve the chances for change. The political stream follows independently of the problem and policy streams. This final stream is similar to motivation or willingness to make policy change and is affected by public mood, campaign dynamics, interest group pressures, election results, partisan makeup of Congress, and administration ideology. Once all three streams are accounted for, one can understand why some worthy issues gain traction and others

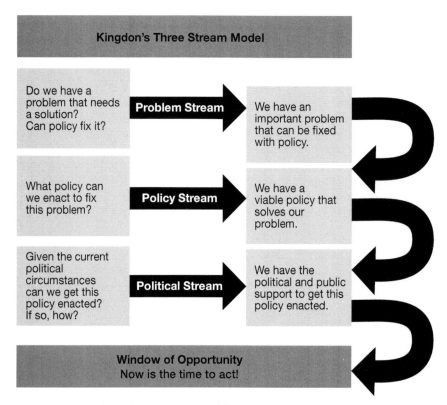

Figure 6.2. Kingdon's Three Streams Model

remain unaddressed. Finding ways to unite these policy streams can help with improved advocacy efforts (Kingdon, 2011).

When considering the problem and policy streams, special educators can learn to bring the right kind of attention to issues needing attention. For starters, when making a policy request, getting goal focused can be helpful for obtaining a yes. Specific goal-oriented solutions with clear, actionable parameters will help inform other stakeholders and pave a clear pathway to forward progress. This also means avoiding increasing others' workloads. Your solution should not become another person's problem. Feasible solutions that are indeed actionable will not put unnecessary strain or burden on others. So in the earlier example of the state shortage in school psychologists, the solution for a shortage in psychologists to conduct triannual evaluations is not to shift that responsibility of such evaluations to another group such as the special education teachers. Increasing special education teachers' workloads will not result in a sustainable solution. Rather, coming with a focused solution that accounts for contextual factors, such as the historical evolution of state licensure requirements for school psychologists, can minimize burden and maximize progress. Instead of shifting burdens, solutions might mean more time transitioning to new state policies or additional supports to help with implementation of new state-level initiatives. Tangible solutions such as additional time and resources can make all the difference.

WHERE CAN I FIND MORE INFORMATION ON STATE-LEVEL ADVOCACY?

CEC State and Provincial Units

 The Council for Exceptional Children gives you access to a local network of professionals by state (United States) and provincial unit (Canada). Follow the link to find contact information for state-level CEC units: https://exceptionalchildren .org/engage/units.

FindLaw.com

 Explore the legal basis behind the hot-button issue of school curriculum development. Articles at the bottom of the page explore other hot-button issues such as curriculum and ideology, Common Core, and sex education in schools. Learn more at https://www.findlaw.com/education/curriculum-standards-school-funding/ school-curriculum-basics.html.

50 State Survey of Special Education Laws and Regulations

 This resource provides laws and regulations for special education by state. The links provided will take you to the statute. Visit https://fclawlib.libguides.com/specialeducation /50statesurvey.

USA.gov

 Provided by the federal government, this resource gives you access to contact information for your governor and state agencies. Visit https://www.usa.gov/states-and-territories.

KEY TERMS

adequate yearly progress: The amount of yearly improvement each school and district are expected to make to enable low-achieving students to meet high performance levels expected of all children.

alternative route program: Nontraditional teacher preparation program designed to train and license people who already have an undergraduate degree in something other than education.

appropriation: A legal authorization to make specified expenditures for specified purposes.

balanced literacy: Explicit language instruction with independent learning and language exploration.

common law: A body of unwritten laws based on legal precedents.

corporal punishment: Physical force used to cause pain or discomfort.

earmarked: Designated for a particular purpose.

hot button: An emotional and usually controversial issue that triggers immediate intense reaction.

oversight: The review, monitoring, inspection, or examination of policy.

phonics: A method of teaching people to read by correlating sounds with letters or groups of letters in an alphabetic writing system.

pinnacle: The highest or most successful point.

policy brief: A concise summary of an issue that includes the policy options to solve a problem and recommendations on the best option.

policy stream: Creating a list of potential proposals for addressing the problem stream influenced by aspects such as feasibility, likelihood of gaining consensus, options for adoption, and anticipation of drawbacks.

political stream: Motivation or willingness to make policy change and is affected by public mood, campaign dynamics, interest group pressures, election results, partisan makeup of Congress, and administration ideology.

problem stream: Existence of a condition is interpreted in a way that requires attention, focus, and action.

science of reading: A vast, interdisciplinary body of scientifically based research about reading and issues related to reading and writing.

traditional preparation program: A four- or five-year undergraduate teacher preparation program at a postsecondary institution.

whole language: A method of teaching children to read at an early age that allows students to select their own reading matter and emphasizes the use and recognition of words in everyday contexts.

DISCUSSION QUESTIONS

1. What are some current state-level advocacy issues in your state?
2. Who are some key state-level education stakeholders in your state? What educational priorities do they hold?
3. How have alternative preparation programs affected the field of special education?
4. In your own words, why is state-level advocacy important?
5. Why should you use Kingdon's (2011) three-stream model when considering state-level advocacy efforts?

REFERENCES

American Rescue Plan Act of 2021, Pub. L. No. 117-2.

Barshay, J. (2020, March). *Four things you need to know about the new reading wars: Evidence backs some phonics and other strategies to help children read in the early elementary years.* The Hechinger Report. https://hechingerreport.org/four-things-you-need-to-know-about-the-new-reading-wars/

Borter, G. (2022, September 22). *Explainer: What 'critical race theory' means and why it's igniting debate.* Reuters. https://www.reuters.com/legal/government/what-critical-race-theory-means-why-its-igniting-debate-2021-09-21/

Brownell, M. T., & Leko, M. M. (2018). Advancing coherent theories of change in special education teacher education research: A response to the special issue on the science of teacher professional development. *Teacher Education and Special Education, 41*(2), 158–168. https://doi.org/10.1177/0888406417748430

Brownell, M. T., Sindelar, P. T., Kiely, M. T., & Danielson, L. C. (2010). Special education teacher quality and preparation: Exposing foundations, constructing a new model. *Exceptional Children, 76*(3), 357–377. https://doi.org/10.1177/001440291007600307

Darling-Hammond, L. (2007, May 2). *Evaluating 'No Child Left Behind': The promise and problems of Bush's education policy. The Nation.* https://www.thenation.com/article/archive/evaluating-no-child-left-behind/

Education for All Handicapped Children Act, Pub. L. No. 94-142, 89 Stat. 773.

Every Student Succeeds Act of 2015, Pub. L. No. 114-95 § 4104.

Fisher, D., Frey, N., & Lapp, D. (2023). Veteran teachers' understanding of "balanced literacy." *Journal of Education, 203*(1), 188–195. https://doi.org/10.1177/00220574211025980

Gershoff, E. T., & Font, S. A. (2016). Corporal punishment in U.S. public schools: Prevalence, disparities in use, and status in state and federal policy. *Social Policy Report, 30*(1). https://www.ncbi.nlm.nih.gov/pmc/articles/PMC5766273/

Gershoff, E. T., Purtell, K. M., & Holas, I. (2015). *Corporal punishment in U.S. public schools: Legal precedents, current practices, and future policy.* Springer.

Individuals with Disabilities Education Act of 2004, 20 U.S.C. § 1400.

Ingraham v. Wright, 430 U.S. 651 (1977).

Kingdon, J. W. (2011). *Agendas, alternatives and public policies* (updated 2nd ed.). Pearson.

Leko, M. M., Brownell, M. T., Sindelar, P. T., & Murphy, K. (2012). Promoting special education preservice teacher expertise. *Focus on Exceptional Children*, *44*(7), 1–16. https://doi.org/10.17161/foec.v44i7.6684

Markelz, A. M., & Bateman, D. F. (2022). *The essentials of special education law.* Rowman & Littlefield.

Nagro, S. A., Markelz, A., Davis, R., & Macedonia, A. (2022). The evolution of access to education for students with disabilities: Landmark legislation, court cases, and policy initiatives that set precedents for the *Gary B.* court decision. *Journal of Disability Policy Studies*, *33*(4), 289–300. https://doi.org/10.1177/10442073221094806

No Child Left Behind Act of 2001, Pub. L. No. 107-110, 30 Stat. 750.

Peyton, D. J., Acosta, K., Harvey, A., Pua, D. J., Sindelar, P. T., Mason-Williams, L., Dewey, J., Fisher, T. L., & Crews, E. (2021). Special education teacher shortage: Differences between high and low shortage states. *Teacher Education and Special Education*, *44*(1), 5–23. https://doi.org/10.1177/0888406420906618

Rosenberg, M. S., Boyer, K. L., Sindelar, P. T., & Misra, S. K. (2007). Alternative route programs for certification in special education: Program infrastructure, instructional delivery, and participant characteristics. *Exceptional Children*, *73*(2), 224–241. https://doi.org/10.1177/001440290707300206

Semingson, P., & Kerns, W. (2021). Where is the evidence? Looking back to Jeanne Chall and enduring debates about the science of reading. *Reading Research Quarterly*, *56*(1), S157–S169. https://doi.org/10.1002/rrq.405

Smith, S. W., & Yell, M. L. (2013). *Preventing problem behavior in the classroom.* Merrill/Pearson Education.

Sutcher, L., Darling-Hammond, L., & Carver-Thomas, D. (2019). Understanding teacher shortages: An analysis of teacher supply and demand in the United States. *Education Policy Analysis Archives*, *27*(35), 1–40. https://files.eric.ed.gov/fulltext/EJ1213618.pdf

US Department of Education. (2022). *National assessment of educational progress (NAEP), various years, 1990–2022 reading assessments*. https://www.nationsreportcard.gov/mathematics/supportive_files/2022_rm_infographic.pdf

Chapter Seven

Ring of Federal Advocacy

The US federal government's involvement in our education system, which formally began in 1965 with the passage of the Elementary and Secondary Education Act (ESEA), is relatively new when considering the US federal government was established in 1789. However, in the past 60 years, the public education system has been shaped by federal initiatives in significant ways. Historically, the federal government's involvement in the education system has centered around offering support for vulnerable student populations including students from low-income families, students with disabilities, and students from immigrant families or other marginalized groups. The federal government began connecting students' academic performance in reading, writing, and mathematics to civil rights issues of poverty and discrimination. This was done with funding decisions that provided grants for overhauling the education system. Federal funding now supports all sectors of education for students ages birth through 21 across curriculum development, educational personnel training, and even infrastructure. The federal government's role in special education was made clear in 1975 with the passage of the Education for All Handicapped Children Act (EAHCA; Public Law 94-142). The EAHCA guaranteed access to education for more than one million children with disabilities previously excluded from formal educational opportunities. Given the influence the federal government has on our education system, it is important to understand how to engage in advocacy at the federal level. Teachers may see themselves far removed from Washington, D.C., but through advocacy at the federal level, individual voices can coalesce to shape the direction of the nation's education system. In chapter 7, we will explore the federal advocacy ring (figure 7.1) and answer these essential questions:

Figure 7.1. The Federal Advocacy Ring

1. What is the federal advocacy ring and why is it important?
2. What are some current opportunities for federal advocacy?
3. How do you advocate at the federal level?
4. Where can I find more information on federal-level advocacy?

WHAT IS THE FEDERAL ADVOCACY RING AND WHY IS IT IMPORTANT?

Each citizen in the United States is a **constituent**, or voting member of their community, with the power to elect representatives to office at the federal level. The 435 elected members in the House of Representatives and the 100 elected members in the Senate combine to form the US Congress (also known as the legislative branch), which is intended to represent the interests of all their constituents across the United States. Congress women and men have to understand their constituents' needs and expectations to properly represent them during the **legislative process**, a process where Congress formally updates old laws, establishes new laws, and allocates money to help with implementing existing laws. Although state laws tend to be more specific than federal laws (see figure 7.2 as an example), the implications of federal policies have the greatest reach across all 50 states and US territories.

As a constituent, you likely make voting decisions based on many personal factors, and regardless of whether you voted for your current elected officials or not, you are still an important part of their constituency. Once in office,

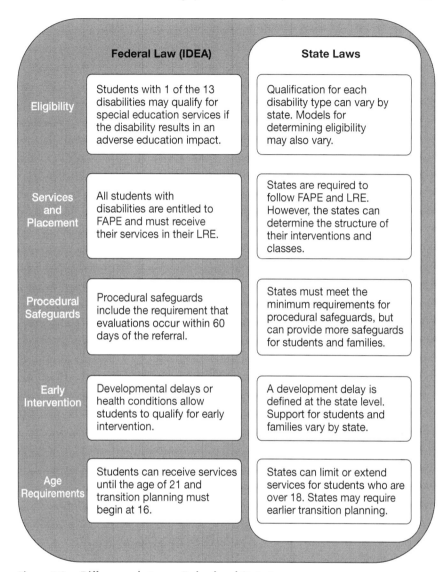

Federal Law (IDEA)	State Laws
Eligibility — Students with 1 of the 13 disabilities may qualify for special education services if the disability results in an adverse education impact.	Qualification for each disability type can vary by state. Models for determining eligibility may also vary.
Services and Placement — All students with disabilities are entitled to FAPE and must receive their services in their LRE.	States are required to follow FAPE and LRE. However, the states can determine the structure of their interventions and classes.
Procedural Safeguards — Procedural safeguards include the requirement that evaluations occur within 60 days of the referral.	States must meet the minimum requirements for procedural safeguards, but can provide more safeguards for students and families.
Early Intervention — Developmental delays or health conditions allow students to qualify for early intervention.	A development delay is defined at the state level. Support for students and families vary by state.
Age Requirements — Students can receive services until the age of 21 and transition planning must begin at 16.	States can limit or extend services for students who are over 18. States may require earlier transition planning.

Figure 7.2.   Differences between Federal and State Laws

elected officials need continuous input from their constituency on current issues. Your expertise in education and understanding of the needs of students with disabilities make you a very useful resource. Your insights can help inform your elected officials as they work on solving education-related problems using the legislative process. This might include sharing your perspective on national politics or local events all with the goal of building understanding around the challenges special education teachers face when trying to meet the diverse needs of students with disabilities and their families.

If you are not telling your story, someone else is. Who better to share stories about the challenges facing special education teachers than special education teachers themselves? When helping to maintain things that are working and improve things that are not through advocating at the federal level, you are not only contributing to solutions for your community but for everyone in the country. Your effect can be wide reaching. The federal government's expanded role in public education is intended to improve student outcomes across the country (Gilmour et al., 2019), and significant aspects of special education are driven by decisions made during the legislative process (Rude & Miller, 2018). Advocacy efforts were vital to the initial passage of landmark special education and disability legislation and continue to be a powerful influence today (Landmark et al., 2016; Yell, 2019). In the past 60 years, special education stakeholders have been able to make a difference in the education of students with disabilities, but the job is still underway.

WHAT ARE SOME CURRENT OPPORTUNITIES FOR FEDERAL ADVOCACY?

In this section, you will learn about some opportunities to advocate at the federal level. The intention is not to tell you where you should land on these issues but rather, to provide some insights into the types of challenges facing our profession today that create opportunities for action.

Funding for IDEA

Since 1975, the EAHCA (now reauthorized as the Individuals with Disabilities Education Act [IDEA, 2004]) has required states to provide a free appropriate public education (FAPE) to eligible students with disabilities. Originally focused on students in grades K–12, the law was expanded in 1986 (i.e., Part C of IDEA) to provide access to early intervention services for infants and toddlers with disabilities and their families and to extend FAPE to preschool-aged children with disabilities. Since then, financial assistance has been provided annually to every state to offer early intervention services, K–12 education services, transition supports, and educator preparation funding for children with disabilities from birth through age 21.

The original intent of the law was to ensure access to education for students with disabilities. When the law was passed in 1975, it had the following provisions: nondiscriminatory identification and evaluation, appropriate education, individualized instruction, education in the least restrictive environment, due process safeguards, and parent participation. To get states to participate, Congress committed to covering 40% of the additional costs of educating children with disabilities in the K–12 setting. However, the current amount of funds provided by Congress is approximately 14.6% of the additional costs in fiscal year 2021 (National Center for Learning Disabilities, 2021).

According to the most recent report to Congress from the Office of Special Education Programs at the Department of Education, there were 427,234 infants and toddlers ages birth through two years served under Part C (US Department of Education, 2021). The same year, there were 806,319 children ages 3–5 served under Part B for preschool services. There were 6,472,061 students with disabilities ages 6–21 served in schools across the United States. This number represents approximately 9.7% of the resident population ages 6–21.

Through IDEA regulations, the federal government provides Part B and Part C formula funding grants to states depending on the number of students with disabilities served. The purpose of this money is as follows:

- To ensure all children with disabilities have available to them FAPE that emphasizes special education and related services designed to meet their unique needs and prepare them for further education, employment, and independent living.
- To ensure the rights of children with disabilities and their parents are protected.
- To assist states, localities, educational service agencies, and federal agencies to provide for the education of all children with disabilities.
- To assess and ensure the effectiveness of efforts to educate children with disabilities.

The distribution of these funds is not without controversy.

Kolbe and colleagues (2022) claim federal special education funding formulas disparately distribute dollars to states. As a result, some states receive more funding per child than others. For example, the difference in IDEA grant amounts between the states at the top and bottom of the distribution in 2022 was about $1,442 per child; Wyoming received about $2,826 for each child receiving special education, and Nevada received $1,384 per child. In other words, for that year federal IDEA funding covered about 23% of the national average additional cost of educating a student with a disability in Wyoming, whereas federal dollars covered about 11% of additional spending in Nevada (Kolbe et al., 2022).

During the 1997 reauthorization of IDEA, Congress updated the funding formula to what it is today. The funding formula is composed of two parts: (1) a base funding amount equivalent to what each state received for fiscal year 1999 and (2) a population-poverty calculation that allocates all new appropriations above the fiscal year 1999 base amount according to states' relative child population and poverty counts for the prior academic year. After these calculations, a state's allocation may be further adjusted to protect states from receiving significantly less funding than the previous year. At the time, there was a minimal difference between state funding. However, fixing dollar amounts to 1999 levels has become increasingly disconnected from changes to states' special education child counts, thus exacerbating funding disproportionality.

To receive IDEA grants, states are required to submit performance plans/ annual performance reports to the US Department of Education every year describing how each state is meeting the requirements of IDEA. Information about the implementation of IDEA across the country is compiled into an annual report to Congress on the indicators required for reporting, which include children served, educational environments, participation and performance in state assessments, information regarding educators, dispute resolution claims, and early intervention services provided.

In addition, states must examine representation of racial and ethnic groups receiving special education and related services that is the result of inappropriate identification. States must report data on significant discrepancies in suspension and expulsion based on race and ethnicity. This reporting stems from the requirements of the equity in IDEA regulation, which requires an examination of data to determine if significant **disproportionality** based on race and ethnicity may be occurring in the state and districts.

All states have the responsibility, under federal law, to have a system of general supervision monitoring the implementation of the IDEA by local school districts. The general supervision system should be accountable for both enforcing procedural requirements and ensuring continuous improvement.

Federal Funding to Support Teachers

In 2007, the federal government passed the College Cost Reduction and Access Act to help "prepare America's youth for the jobs of tomorrow" by expanding access to higher education. This act includes funding for Pell grants, which help offset college costs for low-income students. There are other funds designated within the College Cost Reduction and Access Act (2007) for helping college students afford an education as well (see table 7.1). For example, there is a specific funding program designed for individuals looking to become high-quality teachers in a high-need field called the Teacher Education Assistance for College and Higher Education (TEACH) grants. These TEACH grants were introduced to provide $4,000 a year for

Table 7.1. Federal Funding for Teachers

Funding Program	Details	Website to Learn More
Pell Grants	Up to $6,895 in yearly grant funds awarded to undergraduate students with financial need or post baccalaureate students enrolled in a teacher certification program	https://studentaid.gov/understand-aid/types/grants/pell
Teacher Education Assistance for College and Higher Education (TEACH) Grants	Up to $4,000 in yearly grant funds awarded to students who are completing or plan to complete a teacher preparation program	https://studentaid.gov/understand-aid/types/grants/teach
Public Service Loan Forgiveness (PSLF)	Forgives the remaining balance of federal loans after 120 qualifying payments (estimated over 10 years)	https://studentaid.gov/articles/teacher-loan-forgiveness-options/
Teacher Loan Forgiveness (TLF)	Forgives up to $17,500 of federal Stafford loans after five consecutive years of teaching at a qualifying school	https://studentaid.gov/articles/teacher-loan-forgiveness-options/
Perkins Loan Cancellation for Teachers	Forgives up to 100% of federal Perkins loans: • 15% after first and second years • 20% after third and fourth years • 30% after fifth year	https://studentaid.gov/articles/teacher-loan-forgiveness-options/

teacher candidates seeking licensure to serve low-income students. To be eligible for these funds, teacher candidates have to agree to teach as an elementary or secondary teacher in a high-needs field at a school serving low-income students for four years. These grants are still available today.

Similarly, through the Department of Education, there are currently three federal loan forgiveness programs that allow public school teachers to apply for loan forgiveness after staying in the field of teaching for a designated period of time. First, the Department of Education passed regulations through the Office of Postsecondary Education for Public Service Loan Forgiveness. This program is intended to encourage individuals to enter and remain in teaching roles by forgiving student loans. Second is the Perkins Loan Cancellation for Teachers. This program is a tiered forgiveness program where individuals who teach in special education at a low-income school are eligible for a percentage of their student loans to be forgiven each year they teach. Third is the Teacher Loan Forgiveness (TLF) program. The TLF program forgives up to $17,500 in student loans after an individual teaches as a special educator for five consecutive years at a low-income school. Each of these programs has slightly different rules and guidelines, but they are all examples of federal funding to support the recruitment, preparation, and retention of special education teachers.

Promoting Diversity in Teacher Education

The Augustus F. Hawkins Centers for Excellence Program, authorized under Part B of Title II of the Higher Education Act of 1965, is designed to support centers of excellence at institutions of higher education (IHEs). The selected centers of excellence must be established at Historically Black Colleges and Universities (HBCUs), Tribal Colleges or Universities (TCUs), or Minority Serving Institutions (MSIs). The Hawkins Program's purpose is to help increase the number of well-prepared teachers, including teachers of color, resulting in a more diverse teacher workforce prepared to teach in low-performing elementary and secondary schools to close **achievement gaps**. This federally funded program focuses on various aspects of the teacher preparation pipeline, including the recruitment, preparation, support, placement, and retention of teachers in high-need school districts to support underserved students. Through this program, the Department of Education seeks to fund applicants who propose to incorporate evidence-based components and practices into their teacher preparation program.

Teacher preparation programs at HBCUs, TCUs, and MSIs are long-standing sources of well-prepared and diverse teachers. For example, despite making up just 3% of institutions of higher education, HBCUs prepare 50% of the nation's Black teachers (James et al., 2020). Furthermore, MSIs are responsible for conferring bachelor's degrees in education to nearly half of all Latinx teachers, 35% of Asian Americans, 50% of Pacific Islanders, and 35% of Native Americans (US Department of Education, 2016). Federal funding for the Hawkins Program is quite small compared to other initiatives. For nearly a decade, the program received no financial support. Most recently in fiscal year 2022, the program was allocated approximately $8 million.

Alternative Routes into the Profession

Alternative routes (AR), sometimes called alternate routes to licensure, are pathways to gain state licensure that typically bypass traditional teacher certification requirements, such as coursework and field experiences (Rosenberg & Sindelar, 2005). Teachers who participate in AR programs earn a provisional or emergency license that allows them to serve as the teacher of record while working toward meeting the requirements of professional licensure over a period of time, typically three to five years. Alternative certification programs can be run in a partnership between **local education agencies** (LEAs) and IHEs, where the LEA hires the teachers and the IHE prepares them. Alternative certifications can also consist of privately run, for-profit organizations such as Teachers for Tomorrow or nonprofit organizations such as Teach for America, where recent college graduates are attracted into the profession, prepared by staff internally, and then teach in a high-needs field or classroom for at least two years without any expectation that they become professionally certified. Day (2022) found that AR programs that incorporate IHE support and non-IHE programs produce similar numbers of program completers; however, IHE programs are significantly more likely to include critical preparation components such as field experiences.

Though states and IHEs often fund AR programs and are responsible for their implementation, AR programs are an issue for federal advocacy due to their prevalence across the United States and the increasing reliance on them to fill vacant teaching positions (see chapter 9). Given the abbreviated preparation many AR teachers undergo, concerns regarding teacher quality have caused many to question the success of programs that place teachers into classrooms without complete preparation. No Child Left Behind (2001) required each teacher to be "highly qualified." When the law was reauthorized as the Every Student Succeeds Act (2015), this provision was removed, allowing the proliferation of these programs. Even so, IDEA (2004) requires that special education teachers be adequately and appropriately prepared and certified to teach as special education teachers. The Director of the Office of Special Education Programs made this clear to state directors of special education in a 2022 memo, where she noted, personnel who are participating in a program that provides an alternate route to special education teacher certification must: (1) receive high-quality professional development that is sustained, intensive, and classroom-focused . . .; (2) participate in a program of intensive supervision that consists of structured guidance and regular ongoing support for teachers or a teacher mentoring program; (3) assume the functions as a teacher only for a specified period of time not to exceed three years; and (4) demonstrate satisfactory progress toward full certification as prescribed by the state. (US Department of Education, 2022, p. 2)

Professional development, rigorous induction, ongoing administrative support, and supervision are critical components of effective teacher preparation programs and are particularly important for AR programs. Although IDEA Part B mandates that these facets of teacher preparation be included in AR programs, ensuring that federal requirements are implemented at the state and local levels is undoubtedly an opportunity for advocacy.

HOW DO YOU ADVOCATE AT THE FEDERAL LEVEL?

First, be sure to vote. Advocating at the ballot box is nothing to be overlooked. Beyond voting, there are many ways in which one can advocate at the federal level. You can begin as a well-informed individual. Then, you can find other individuals to form organizations or special interest groups. There are many well-known special education organizations such as the Council for Exceptional Children (CEC) and the National Association of Special Education Teachers (NASET). These organizations and interest groups come together to partner with one another around shared issues to create **coalitions**. A coalition is a group of allied parties seeking combined action around a common issue. For example, the National Coalition on Personnel Shortages in Special Education and Related Services (NCPSSERS) is a national coalition composed of more than 30 participating member organizations, allied around the issue of personnel shortages in special education and related services. Soon, you have the power of numbers.

Identify and Understand the Problem

In one sense, identifying and understanding the problem will come naturally to most special education teachers who live the challenges of the profession each day. Experiencing federal policies in practice at the classroom level can make special education teachers uniquely qualified to help others understand the outcomes (sometimes unintended) of both good and bad federal policy decisions. The next step is to seek out reliable information channels through professional organizations to better understand if these challenges have implications at the federal level. Not all problems will have federal solutions, but in many cases the struggles in one classroom or school district are also being experienced by many classrooms and districts across the country. Conferring with trusted sources such as briefs, position papers, and peer-reviewed publications from professional organizations, associations, and networks whose mission you share is a great place to search for understanding.

Invite Stakeholders

One aspect of understanding is identifying whether an issue has momentum. Many professional organizations will organize campaigns to raise awareness to gain the attention of policy makers by first gaining the attention of their constituents. When the general public becomes aware and voices serious concern, you have momentum that can initiate change at the federal level. Those issues that extend beyond grade-level meetings or district updates and find themselves on the nightly news or being discussed in popular press outlets can draw attention from an array of stakeholders including other teachers and school personnel, families, community leaders, and elected officials.

Organizing around an issue requires planning and infrastructure. Coalitions usually have an infrastructure in place that encourages stakeholders to sign onto letters, attend town halls, make congressional visits, respond to calls for public comment, and continue to give attention to the problems needing solutions. Seeking your like-minded stakeholders through professional organizations and then encouraging your professional organizations to engage in advocacy work at the federal level is a worthwhile endeavor. Again, there is power in numbers. Bringing stakeholders together means one letter to a senator serving on the Senate Committee on Health, Education, Labor, and Pensions (HELP) can represent 1,000 members' voices from an organization or even 10,000 members' voices from a coalition. Think about what it means to have 10,000 tally marks in the "make a change column" on a senator's morning memo as they prepare for their committee meeting later that day.

Determine Solutions

Advocating at the federal level is a bit like finding the moving train and hitching your boxcar to it. Last year, 16,601 bills were introduced in Congress, and only 2%, or 344, of those bills were **enacted legislation**, which means they were signed into law by the president or a veto was overridden (GovTrack, 2022). Further complicating things, major legislation like ESSA (2015) and IDEA (2004) seem like trains collecting dust in the rail yard. Hitching your solution to a major piece of legislation may not be the best approach to finding timely solutions. The good news is that of the 344 bills passed last year, there were some smaller bills, such as the Lifespan Respite Care Program, aimed at helping caregivers of individuals with disabilities. Problems related to special education and disability services were remedied within that smaller bill. Advocating through multiple channels by supporting several smaller bills in the hopes that your solution attaches itself to enacted legislation can require some strategizing.

Most professional organizations have **government relations professionals** including consultants and volunteers to stay abreast of the current happenings on Capitol Hill. Government relations professionals work specifically to advocate for the needs of the group they represent by persuading government officials to change or maintain policies that align with their organization's identified solutions. These folks are not necessarily the content experts. They depend on organization members to be the valuable resource of experience and understanding. In collaboration with the organization and on behalf of its members, government relations professionals seek out viable pathways for solutions or offer suggestions for how to promote awareness and understanding as a first step toward paving the pathway for national change. Some professional organizations put out action alerts to notify members of opportunities to lend their voice to a solution. This might include sending emails, making phone calls, providing comments or feedback on a bill or hearing, or visiting with elected officials to discuss an issue. Enrolling in action alerts and opting in for government relations newsletters or updates are great options for determining viable outlets for advocacy.

WHERE CAN I FIND MORE INFORMATION ON FEDERAL-LEVEL ADVOCACY?

Advocating for the Common Good: People, Politics, Process, and Policy on Capitol Hill

 Dr. Jane West, a special education policy consultant and advocate, examines the four Ps—people, politics, process, and policy—and describes how an understanding of all four can aid your advocacy and make meaningful change. Learn more at https://rowman .com/ISBN/9781538155226/Advocating-for-the-Common-Good-People -Politics-Process-and-Policy-on-Capitol-Hill.

Individuals with Disabilities Education Act Site

Administered by the US Department of Education, this website provides details on the history and implementation of IDEA. Visit https://sites.ed.gov/idea/.

Policy Insider

The CEC's Policy Insider blog will keep you informed of important changes to special education policy and law at the federal level. Many of the blog posts center on guidance from the Office of Special Education Programs, a discussion of hot-button issues, and updates regarding the implementation of IDEA. Visit https://exceptionalchildren.org/policy-insider.

Special Education Legislative Summit

Each year the Council for Special Education organizes an opportunity for members to lobby their congressional representatives regarding issues affecting students with disabilities, their families, and their teachers. Consider attending or learning more. Visit https://specialeducationlegislativesummit.org/.

Your Voice Matters: A Practitioner's Guide for Engaging in Policy through Advocacy

In this 2020 article, the authors discuss how policy affects systems and practices, summarize foundations for understanding policy, and provide a scaffolded approach for special education professionals to engage in policy and advocacy. Access this article at https://journals.sagepub.com/doi/10.1177/1096250620950311.

KEY TERMS

achievement gaps: Persistent disparities in measures of educational performance among subgroups of US students, especially groups defined by socioeconomic status, race/ethnicity, and gender.

coalition: A group of allied parties seeking combined action around a common issue.

constituent: Voting member of a given community with the power to elect representatives to office.

disproportionality: The overrepresentation or underrepresentation of groups of students in comparison to their share of the general population.

enacted legislation: Bills that were signed into law by the president or a veto was overridden.

government relations professionals: Individuals who work specifically on advocating for the needs of the group they represent by persuading government officials to change or maintain policies that align with their organization's identified solutions.

legislative process: A process where Congress formally updates old laws, establishes new laws, and allocates money to help with implementing existing laws.

local education agency: A board of education or other public authority legally constituted within a state to serve as an administrative agency for its public schools.

DISCUSSION QUESTIONS

1. What are some obstacles to advocating within the federal ring of advocacy?
2. Who are your federal government senators and representatives? What are their stated policies on education/special education?
3. What are the benefits and drawbacks of alternative route programs to licensure?
4. In your own words, why is federal-level advocacy important?
5. What current federal advocacy opportunity interests you? How would you advocate for this issue?

REFERENCES

College Cost Reduction and Access Act of 2007, Pub. L. No. 110-84, 10 U.S.C. § 101.

Day, J. (2022). *Alternate route programs and special education teacher preparation* [Unpublished doctoral dissertation]. George Mason University.

Education for All Handicapped Children Act of 1975, Pub. L. No. 94-142, 89 Stat. 773.

Elementary and Secondary Education Act of 1965, Pub. L. No. 89-10, § 79 Stat. 27.

Every Student Succeeds Act of 2015, Pub. L. No. 114-95 § 4104.

Gilmour, A. F., Fuchs, D., & Wehby, J. H. (2019). Are students with disabilities accessing the curriculum? A meta-analysis of the reading achievement gap between students with and without disabilities. *Exceptional Children, 85*(3), 329–346.

GovTrack. (2022). *Statistics and historical comparison.* https://www.govtrack.us/congress/bills/statistics

Higher Education Act of 1965, Pub. L. No. 89-329, 20 U.S.C. § 1001 et seq.

Individuals with Disabilities Education Act of 2004, 20 U.S.C. § 1400.

James, W., Scott, L., & Temple, P. (2020). Strategies used by historically Black colleges and universities to recruit minority teacher education candidates. *Teacher Educators' Journal, 13*, 76–104. https://files.eric.ed.gov/fulltext/EJ1247296.pdf

Kolbe, T., Dhuey, E., & Doutre, S. M. (2022). More money is not enough: (Re)considering policy proposals to increase federal funding for special education. *American Journal of Education, 129*(1), 79–108. https://www.journals.uchicago.edu/doi/abs/10.1086/721846

Landmark, L. J., Zhang, D., Ju, S., McVey, T. C., & Ji, M. Y. (2016). Experiences of disability advocates and self-advocates in Texas. *Journal of Disability Policy Studies, 27*, 203–211.

National Center for Learning Disabilities. (2021). *IDEA full funding: Why should Congress invest in special education?* https://ncld.org/news/policy-and-advocacy/idea-full-funding-why-should-congress-invest-in-special-education/

No Child Left Behind Act of 2001, Pub. L. No. 107-110, 30 Stat. 750.

Rosenberg, M. S., & Sindelar, P. T. (2005). The proliferation of alternative routes to certification in special education: A critical review of the literature. *Journal of Special Education, 39*(2), 117–127. https://doi.org/10.1177/00224669050390020201

Rude, H., & Miller, K. J. (2018). Policy challenges and opportunities for rural special education. *Rural Special Education Quarterly, 37*, 21–29. https://doi.org/10.1177/8756870517748662

US Department of Education. (2016, July). *The state of racial diversity in the educator* workforce. http://www2.ed.gov/rschstat/eval/highered/racial-diversity/state-racial-diversity-workforce.pdf

US Department of Education. (2021, January). *43rd annual report to Congress on the implementation of the Individuals with Disabilities Education Act, 2021.* https://sites.ed.gov/idea/files/43rd-arc-for-idea.pdf

US Department of Education. (2022, October 4). *Personnel qualifications under part B of the Individuals with Disabilities Education Act (IDEA).* https://sites.ed.gov/idea/files/OSEP-Memo-22-01-Personnel-Qualifications-under-IDEA-10-04-2022.pdf

Yell, M. L. (2019). *The law and special education* (5th ed.). Pearson.

ADVOCACY IN PRACTICE

Chapter Eight

Inclusion of Students with Disabilities

Prior to the passage of the Education for All Handicapped Children Act (EAHCA, 1975), the inclusion of students with disabilities in public school was limited. The few students who did receive public education were often taught in poor facilities that were segregated from the general population. To address this inequity, Congress adopted a measure in the final passage of EAHCA to prevent the educational segregation of students with disabilities. Known as the least restrictive environment (LRE) mandate, schools were now required to educate students with disabilities alongside their nondisabled peers to the maximum extent appropriate. Although it took several years, case laws, and regulatory guidance, the LRE mandate has been instrumental in incorporating students with disabilities into general education classrooms. In addition, the meaning of inclusion has evolved from a concept of *access to* general education classrooms to *achievement in* the general education curriculum (Nagro et al., 2022). Yet even with the progress that has been made, issues concerning the inclusion of students with disabilities persist. It was mentioned in earlier chapters that there is a debate growing about the purpose of LRE and what inclusion should mean for students with disabilities. As this debate unfolds, special education teachers should advocate to shape this issue for the benefit of their students. The purpose of the next three chapters in this book is to focus on particular topics and demonstrate how special education teachers can use the five rings of advocacy (figure 8.1) to effect change. Although we select solutions to advocate for in the provided examples, it is not our intention to impose a specific philosophy, organizing principle, or solution. The complexity of these issues and variety of contextual factors mean it is up to you, the educator, to understand nuances and determine what to advocate for. We simply hope to provide examples of how specific

Figure 8.1. The Five Rings of Advocacy

opportunities for advocacy can be addressed. In chapter 8, we will explore the topic of inclusion and address these essential questions:

1. What are the issues concerning inclusion of students with disabilities?
2. How do you use the rings of advocacy concerning issues of inclusion?
3. Where can I find more information about inclusion?

WHAT ARE THE ISSUES CONCERNING INCLUSION OF STUDENTS WITH DISABILITIES?

Because the Individuals with Disabilities Education Act (IDEA, 2004) does not mention "inclusion," any special education law textbook or discussion about inclusion is going to pivot around LRE (e.g., Brady et al., 2019; Markelz & Bateman, 2022; Yell, 2019). As one of the main gears of IDEA, LRE has been a topic of debate for many years (Kauffman, Anastasiou, et al., 2022). The **catalyst** of this controversy deals with the definition of LRE. According to IDEA:

> To the maximum extent appropriate, children with disabilities, including children in public or private institutions or other care facilities, are educated with children who are not disabled, and that special classes, separate schooling, or other removal of children with disabilities from the regular educational environment occurs only when the nature or severity of the disability is such that

education in regular classes with the use of supplementary aids and services cannot be achieved.

It is clear within the IDEA definition of LRE that the preferred setting for students with disabilities is alongside students without disabilities. Subjectivity enters the discussion when words are used such as "maximum extent appropriate" and "severity of the disability is such that education in the regular class with use of supplementary aids and services cannot be achieved."

Based on interpretations, imprecise use of the term has contributed to the debate about what LRE means. Is a student's LRE always the general education classroom where they are closest to nondisabled peers? Or does a student's LRE depend on individual circumstances and the success of supplementary aids and services? As introduced in chapter 4, case law has not clarified the definition because US circuit courts have interpreted the language differently. Since the US Supreme Court has not ruled on a case concerning LRE, placement decisions are subject to different "tests" that US circuit courts have developed. Table 8.1 lists the four tests that have been established to guide educators when determining placement.

The US Supreme Court has ruled that a student's free appropriate public education (FAPE) is the primary objective concerning IDEA (2004) adherence (*Endrew F. v. Douglas County School District* [2017]). Therefore, when examining whether placement in the general education classroom is appropriate, individualized education program (IEP) team members must determine whether FAPE can be provided. If not, a more restrictive setting is appropriate. In other words, schools must consider providing special education services in the LRE (i.e., general education classroom) first; however, the appropriateness of that setting for the student's educational progress is more important than the restrictiveness. Given that the general education classroom may not be the most appropriate setting for all students with disabilities, IDEA established a **continuum of placements** to meet the educational needs of all students. To clarify the potential tension between LRE and FAPE, some scholars have suggested a term more useful than LRE is the least restrictive *appropriate* environment (Yell & Prince, 2022). The least restrictive appropriate environment requires the IEP team to consider students' progress toward their IEP goals through the use of special education services while being educated in the placement that will confer FAPE (Yell & Prince, 2022).

To complicate matters, competing ideologies about inclusion and interpretations of LRE have emerged among scholars and stakeholders. This debate is rooted in the historical discrimination of people with disabilities. On one side, there are scholars who are advocating for a **full inclusion movement** (FIM) in which LRE should be moot and that total inclusion of all students with disabilities in general education classes should be required (Slee, 2018;

Table 8.1.   Circuit Court Tests When Determining Least Restrictive Environment

Roncker Test US Circuit Courts: 6th & 8th	Questions to consider when determining LRE placement: 1. Can the educational services that make a more restrictive placement appropriate be feasibly provided in a less restrictive placement? 2. If so, the placement in the more restrictive setting is inappropriate.
Daniel Test US Circuit Courts: 2nd, 3rd, 5th, 10th, & 11th	Questions to consider when determining LRE placement: 1. Can education in the general education classroom with supplementary aids and services be achieved satisfactorily? 2. If a student is placed in a more restrictive setting, is the student integrated to the maximum extent appropriate?
Rachel Test US Circuit Court: 9th	Factors to consider when determining LRE placement: 1. The educational benefits of the general education classroom with supplementary aids and services as compared with the educational benefits of the special classroom. 2. The nonacademic benefits of the interaction with students without disabilities. 3. The effect of the student's presence on the teacher and on other students in the classroom. 4. The cost of inclusion.
DeVries Test US Circuit Court: 4th	Placement in the general education classroom is not required when: 1. A student with a disability would not receive educational benefit from inclusion in a general education class. 2. Any marginal benefit from inclusion would be significantly outweighed by benefits that could feasibly be obtained only in a separate instructional setting. 3. The student is a disruptive force in the general education classroom.

Adapted from Markelz & Bateman (2022).

SWIFT Schools, 2022, Taylor, 2004, 2016). Proponents of the FIM point to the civil rights movement of *Brown v. Board of Education* (1954) and how discrimination and segregation of racial minorities was expanded to confront discrimination and segregation of students with disabilities.

On the other side, scholars suggest that conflating the civil rights of students of color with that of students with disabilities disregards the individuality of disability. Inclusion is very often a good thing but can be taken to harmful extremes (Kauffman, Burke, et al., 2022). Educating students with disabilities in public education is unquestionably a positive development; however, there is a difference between being present in a classroom and receiving an appropriate education. Scholars who support a continuum of placements emphasize the value of educational progress, as individually determined by IEP teams, over proximity to nondisabled students (Yell & Prince, 2022).

In 1989, The US First Circuit Court ruled in *Timothy W. v. Rochester* that all children are educable and affirmed the **zero reject principle** of EAHCA (1975). Even with Timothy's multiple and profound cognitive and physical disabilities, the court ruled that he could benefit from education. Since then, no case has challenged the educable rights of any child with a disability. The uniqueness of Timothy's medical and educational needs highlights the range in circumstances that schools are required to meet and confer FAPE. One aspect that must remain in consideration is the practical implications of ideological debates. Given Timothy's extensive supportive needs and many other students like him, absolute ideological exercises can quickly bump into implementation realities. Should Timothy's educational placement, regardless of his ability to succeed in that environment, be determined by mandated policies? Or should the IEP team reasonably calculate his IEP, considering a continuum of placements, to ensure appropriate educational progress occurs in light of his individual circumstances?

There are many nuances to ideological debates, yet over time these shifts in societal values are how educational policies evolve. The previous section was to inform special education teachers of theoretical movements around the inclusion of students with disabilities. In the next section, we examine with a fictional vignette how one can advocate across the rings of advocacy for a specific situation concerning a change in school policy around inclusive practices.

HOW DO YOU USE THE RINGS OF ADVOCACY CONCERNING ISSUES OF INCLUSION?

Mr. Jacobs is a middle school special education teacher in a rural school that serves approximately 250 students. He has been teaching for five years and feels like he is comfortable with his schedule, caseload, and curriculums. Ever since he was hired at Loveland Middle School, Mr. Jacobs has been a resource room teacher where he pulls out students with specific learning disabilities to provide extra reading and math instruction for 120 minutes a day. Because Mr. Jacobs has 35 students on his caseload, he instructs students that are similar in reading and math abilities across age ranges. Even though his students are in sixth through eighth grade, most of them have been assessed at the first- through fourth-grade academic levels. It is difficult to provide individualized instruction geared toward the general education curriculum across grade levels, but Mr. Jacobs likes that he has his own classroom with established rules and procedures. In his experience, overly crowded general education classrooms are often disruptive and not conducive to learning. He knows the general education teachers are doing their best; however, he is happy to pull out his students to a quieter environment where he can focus on reading and math instruction that is on his students' academic levels.

At the beginning of Mr. Jacobs's sixth year, his special education director informs him and the other special education teachers that the school district is considering a full inclusion model. Apparently, the state education department has been looking at LRE reporting and determined that too many students are receiving education outside the general education classroom. Schools are to adopt co-teaching models so that instead of pulling students out of the general education classroom, Mr. Jacobs will provide instruction alongside general education teachers. This policy shift is not a mandate from the state Department of Education; however, his special education director has been advocating for full inclusion for years. School personnel are given a couple of weeks to figure out how to transition to a co-teaching model and to amend IEPs accordingly.

The Problem

When school- or district-wide policy changes like this are recommended, there can be an immediate resistance to change. It is natural to oppose significant shifts to "how things are normally done." Mr. Jacobs recognizes this reaction within himself. After initial hesitancy, he examines his beliefs about the policy change. He first thinks about the conflicts in scheduling this will create. Rather than being able to pull students at various times to provide reading and math instruction, he will have to be present in general education classrooms when reading and math instruction are taking place. With three classes per grade, what used to be one 60-minute class where he pulled students from those three classes, he now has to split his time across those three classes to be with each of his students. Mr. Jacobs recognizes that providing the required 120 minutes per each student's IEP is going to be difficult.

Mr. Jacobs is also thinking about the present levels of some of his students. For those who are multiple grade levels below their age-appropriate peers, he does not believe the general education classroom is where they can succeed academically. Mr. Jacob believes that inclusion is a great thing, but at the same time, he realizes that some of his students might become frustrated without time to receive more individualized instruction in an environment with a lot fewer students and distractions. If fact, he recently read a book about disability and was introduced to the term **ableism** (Ladau, 2021). Although contrary to what people might initially think, after giving it some thought, Mr. Jacobs believes full inclusion mandates are ableist because they assume students with disabilities must be with nondisabled peers to succeed. If everyone must be educated in the general education classroom, then the assumption is that the general education classroom is the "normal" environment, which is the "right" place for students with disabilities to be educated. To Mr. Jacobs, this line of thinking actually perpetuates **deficit mindset** policies.

Finally, Mr. Jacobs thinks about his students with challenging behaviors. His school is within the Fourth US Circuit Court of Appeals, which means IEP teams are guided by the DeVries Test when determining placement. Within the DeVries Test, student behavior can be considered when determining placement. The test specifically states that inclusion is not required when the student is a disruptive force in the general education classroom (*DeVries v. Fairfax County School Board*, 1989). Mr. Jacobs can immediately think of a few students on his caseload whom he can imagine having a "disruptive nature" if they were required to spend 100% of the school day in the general education classroom. He is not sure full inclusion would meet their academic or behavioral needs.

Mr. Jacobs's Solution

Mr. Jacobs realizes that his first reaction to completely resist the policy change is not helpful. Upon consideration, he feels like he understands a variety of problems with the co-teaching initiative and is ready to advocate for solutions. Mr. Jacobs now recognizes that the current pull-out model has similar problems to the proposed co-teaching model. Neither model, with their **absolutism**, allows for an individualized approach to placement. In fact, pulling out every student for 120 minutes a day for reading and math instruction is guilty of predetermination, just like full inclusion predetermines the general education classroom as placement. Mr. Jacobs decides to advocate for an individualized approach to determining his students' placement and the special education services they require. He believes some students would do well fully included in the general education curriculum with push-in supports and services, while others still need pull-out services to meet their IEP goals.

Rings of Advocacy

Now that Mr. Jacobs has an overall solution to advocate *for*, he needs to identify how to advocate for this solution and whom to advocate *to*. By using the Five Rings of Advocacy Framework (figure 8.1), Mr. Jacobs can organize his advocacy and specifically tailor his efforts across appropriate spheres of influence.

Self-Advocacy Ring

The first step to any advocacy effort is to identify and understand the problem. Within the problem section above, Mr. Jacobs examined the problem from a nonreactionary perspective. He knows the shift in policy is a recommendation from state-level policy makers to increase the number of students receiving services in general education classrooms. He also knows his special education director supports the policy shift from a philosophical standpoint. If implemented as stated, he believes the policy would create several practical complications and not be what is best for all of his students.

Starting at the innermost ring, self-advocacy is about promoting one's own interests. If Mr. Jacobs is going to advocate for a more nuanced approach to student placement, as opposed to 100% pull-out or 100% inclusion, he needs to identify what he wants to advocate for concerning his personal interests. Knowing that some students will be included in the general education classroom full-time, Mr. Jacobs will need to provide services in that setting. This means co-teaching for some of the day will become a new role. Co-teaching is not an instructional practice that is easily adopted and implemented. In fact, effective co-teaching takes a lot of time, planning, collaboration, and practice (Friend, 2018). Therefore, the general education teachers whom he will co-teach with will be important stakeholders concerning these discussions. If co-teaching is going to be successful and he is to avoid being relegated to the classroom assistant role, Mr. Jacobs knows that he will need to advocate for clear co-teaching expectations and sufficient planning time every week to discuss and differentiate lessons.

A second personal issue is **caseload manageability**. Currently, Mr. Jacobs has students across every grade level on his caseload. Given the number of grades (i.e., sixth through eighth) and classes per grade, it does not seem possible to provide services to all his students. One solution might be to reassign caseloads to match grade levels to align schedules better. This way he could be in general education classrooms for some students, while also be able to pull out those who still need services in a more restrictive environment. Since every special education teacher in the building is going to be affected by this policy, Mr. Jacobs knows they will all be important stakeholders when it comes to discussing solutions to scheduling and caseload manageability.

Classroom Advocacy Ring

After thinking about his own personal interests, Mr. Jacobs thinks about the needs of his students. All of his students currently are in the general education classroom most of the day; the only change is that some of them are going to be in the general education classroom all of the day. Unfortunately, one persistent challenge to inclusion is that general education teachers feel unprepared to teach students with disabilities (Blanton et al., 2011). Sometimes an attitude of "those are not my students" develops among general education teachers, and instead of using instructional and behavioral practices to include students with IEPs in the classroom, the general education teacher sends the student to the special education teacher to "deal with." If more of Mr. Jacobs's students are going to be included full-time in the general education class and curriculum, he knows advocacy efforts are needed to ensure that those students are fully included and not simply relegated to tables in the back of the classroom. General education teachers will need to understand their responsibility to develop relationships with these students, provide instruction to meet lesson objectives, ensure FAPE is provided as identified in the IEP, and discipline as needed. Of course, Mr. Jacobs will be present during co-teaching times or available for differentiation support, but there cannot be a difference in treatment between special education students and general education students.

A solution to address the resistance of general education teachers to see students with IEPs as their students, too, is professional development opportunities. To support the transition of this policy, the school could provide professional development sessions on inclusive best practices, such as co-teaching strategies, differentiating reading and math instruction, or evidence-based behavioral practices for working with students who are below grade level academically. Any general education teacher who will now instruct students with IEPs, therefore, will be important stakeholders. In addition, school administrators or personnel responsible for professional development will also need to be included in conversations.

Because some student placements will be changing from resource room instruction to general education classroom instruction, the parents/legal guardians are important stakeholders in these decisions. Parents/legal guardians are required members of the IEP team. Any change in the IEP as significant as an LRE placement change must be approved by them. It is important for the IEP team to convene and discuss each student independently, taking into consideration their individual strengths and needs.

Each interaction with stakeholders is an opportunity for advocacy. While Mr. Jacobs is understanding the implications of the policy shift to full inclusion, he is having conversations with other special education and general education teachers. He is gauging other stakeholders' reactions to the policy shift and is assessing whether there is support for his solutions to look at full inclusion for some students but not all. When it comes time to discuss solutions with stakeholders, it is essential to have (1) solutions for the problem and (2) coalition momentum in support of your solutions.

School Advocacy Ring

The initial policy recommendation came from the state level; however, it was the special education director who suggested the district move toward a full inclusion/co-teaching model. Based on where the policy is coming from (i.e., the director), Mr. Jacobs identifies the school advocacy ring as a very important sphere of influence concerning this policy shift.

Mr. Jacobs has done a lot of work up to this point in examining the new policy, understanding implementation concerns, and strategizing solutions. These are all important steps to identifying and understanding the problem. It is now time to invite stakeholders together and begin working on solutions with change agents. In this scenario, Mr. Jacobs's special education director is the primary change agent since they are requiring the policy shift. The principal of the school is also an important change agent since they have ultimate authority over the school building. Through conversations with the principal, Mr. Jacobs discovers that they are hesitant to the new policy given the problems it will create with scheduling and potential behavior challenges for general education teachers.

When it comes to inviting stakeholders to begin discussing solutions, there are many ways to approach it. Should everyone attend a meeting at once? Should there be a few meetings with change agents first, before bringing in additional stakeholders? There is no right answer to how best to approach this. The problem, solution, and school contextual factors should drive decision-making. For this scenario, Mr. Jacobs believes a meeting with the special education director, principal, and lead general education teacher is a good place to start.

Mr. Jacobs comes prepared to the meeting, confident in his understanding of the problem and abilities to lead the meeting in an effective manner. He has teacher and student schedules available to reference during the conversation. He has data for how many teachers support full inclusion, support the current way of 100% pull-out, and his solution of a middle ground. He also has a couple of examples of students and their IEPs that would benefit from the new policy and a couple that would not benefit.

One of the main points Mr. Jacobs hopes to convey during the initial meeting is that full inclusion, without individual consideration of student need, is just as guilty of predetermination as the current 100% pull-out policy. Reassessing students' placement needs and making determinations on an individual basis is a more legally defensible action. Mr. Jacobs always knew that some students could benefit from a more inclusive placement and that having that compromise ready, is a smart negotiation tactic concerning advocacy.

State Advocacy Ring

Regarding this fictional vignette, the majority of advocacy work is associated with the first three rings of influence. State policy makers did make the recommendation to increase the percentage of students receiving special education services in the general education classroom, but it was the special education director who required the full inclusion model solution. Given Mr. Jacobs's newfound experience with this issue, he wants to continue his advocacy efforts to more expansive spheres of influence. He does a little research into who the state special education director is and what their guiding principles are. He also attends a state public forum where various issues are discussed and there is time for public comment. Mr. Jacobs follows the five-step approach to delivering a message (see chapter 6) when it is his turn to comment. He personally shares that some of his students have really benefited from reexamining their placement and have excelled in the general education classroom. He also shares that a more restrictive placement is beneficial to some of his students, too. He closes his statement by emphasizing the importance of a continuum of placements to meet the needs of each student individually so that an appropriate education is possible for all.

Federal Advocacy Ring

Mr. Jacobs's advocacy work makes him realize the importance of being "at the table." He joins the Council for Exceptional Children (CEC) to be a member of a trusted coalition. He wants to follow federal special education policy actions more closely so that he can make his voice heard on issues. He also wants to become a more educated voting constituent. With CEC membership, Mr. Jacobs has access to resources and other professionals who he did not know existed. Being part of a larger movement of professionals is both invigorating and inspiring. Mr. Jacobs now attends the annual CEC conference to network and professionally develop as a special education teacher.

In Conclusion

As first defined in chapter 2, advocacy is about promoting the interest or cause of someone or a group of people. There are countless issues that special education teachers can advocate for in terms of students with disabilities or the profession as a whole. Based on these incalculable factors, it is difficult to identify a right or wrong way to advocate. We hope the five advocacy rings (figure 8.1) serve as a framework for positioning particular issues. Each ring can serve as a lens to identify and understand the issue, recognize relevant stakeholders, and formulate solutions.

WHERE CAN I FIND MORE INFORMATION ABOUT INCLUSION?

2TeachLLC Blog

A blog that shares best practices and resources for co-teaching. Consider exploring the website to find helpful downloads including co-teaching lesson plans. Visit https://2teachllc.com/blog.

Intervention in School and Clinic

An academic journal geared toward teachers and practitioners. It provides practical tips, techniques, methods, and ideas for supporting students with learning disabilities and behavioral disorders. Learn more at https://journals.sagepub.com/home/isc.

IRIS Center Information Brief: LRE

The IRIS Center at Vanderbilt University provided this informative brief regarding the essential components of the LRE principle of IDEA. It describes, in detail, the continuum of placements as well as measures for determining a child's appropriate placement. View this document at https://iris.peabody.vanderbilt.edu/wp-content/uploads/pdf_info_briefs/IRIS_Least_Restrictive_Environment_InfoBrief_092519.pdf.

Six Co-Teaching Models

Understood.com outlines the six co-teaching models: team teaching; parallel teaching; station teaching; alternative teaching; one teach, one assist; and one teach, one observe. The authors are sure to describe both the benefits and challenges of each model. Visit https://www.understood.org/en/articles/6-models-of-co-teaching.

KEY TERMS

ableism: Discrimination in favor of able-bodied people.

absolutism: A theory holding that values, principles, and actions are not relative, dependent, or changeable.

deficit mindset: A perspective of student ability that focuses on problems, rather than potential.

caseload manageability: The ability to successfully perform the tasks required to ensure FAPE is provided to each student on one's caseload.

catalyst: A person, thing, or event that provokes or speeds significant action or change.

continuum of placements: A spectrum of educational settings where a student's special education program can be implemented.

full inclusion movement: A belief that all students with disabilities should receive special education services in general education classrooms.

zero reject principle: A component of special education law that states schools are responsible for the education of all students with disabilities regardless of nature and severity.

DISCUSSION QUESTIONS

1. Describe the debate between supporters of a continuum of placements and supporters of the full inclusion movement.
2. How could case law clarify subjectivity in IDEA's definition of LRE?
3. What do you think of Mr. Jacobs's advocacy efforts?
4. How would you use the five rings of advocacy to advocate in a similar situation?
5. What experiences have you had with inclusive special education practices?

REFERENCES

Blanton, L. P., Pugach, M. C., & Florian, L. (2011). *Preparing general education teachers to improve outcomes for students with disabilities.* National Center for Learning Disabilities. https://www.ncld.org/wp-content/uploads/2014/11/aacte_ncld _recommendation.pdf

Brady, K. P., Russo, C. J., Dieterich, C. A., & Osborne, A. G., Jr. (2019). *Legal issues in special education: Principles, policies, and practices.* Routledge.

Brown v. Board of Education, 347 U.S. 483 (1954).

DeVries v. Fairfax County School Board, 853 F.2d 264 (4th Cir. 1989).

Education for All Handicapped Children Act of 1975, Pub. L. No. 94-142, 89 Stat. 773.

Endrew F. v. Douglas County School District, 137 S. Ct. 988 (2017).

Friend, M. (2018). *Co-teach! Building and sustaining effective classroom partnerships in inclusive schools* (3rd ed.). Marilyn Friend, Inc.

Individuals with Disabilities Education Act of 2004, 20 U.S.C. § 1400.

Kauffman, J. M., Anastasiou, D., Felder, M., Hornby, G., & Lopes, J. (2022). Recent debates in special and inclusive education. In R. Tierney, F. Rizvi, K. Ercikan, G. Smith, & R. Slee (Eds.), *International encyclopedia of education* (4th ed.). Elsevier.

Kauffman, J. M., Burke, M. D., & Anastasiou, D. (2022). Hard LRE choices in the era of inclusion: Rights and their implications. *Journal of Disability Policy Studies.* https://doi.org/10.1177/10442073221113074

Ladau, E. (2021). *Demystifying disability: What to know, what to say, and how to be an ally.* Ten Speed Press.

Markelz, A. M., & Bateman, D. F. (2022). *The essentials of special education law.* Rowman & Littlefield.

Nagro, S. A., Markelz, A., Davis, R., & Macedonia, A. (2022). The evolution of access to education for students with disabilities: Landmark legislation, court cases, and policy initiatives that set precedents for the *Gary B.* court decision. *Journal of Disability Policy Studies, 33*(4), 289–300. https://doi.org/10.1177/10442073221094806

Slee, R. (2018). *Inclusive education isn't dead, it just smells funny.* Routledge.

SWIFT Schools. (2022). https://swiftschools.org

Taylor, S. J. (2004). Caught in the continuum: A critical analysis of the principle of least restrictive environment. *Research and Practice for Persons with Severe Disabilities, 29*(4), 218–230. https://doi.org/10.2511/rpsd.29.4.218

Taylor, S. J. (2016). Still caught in the continuum: A critical analysis of least restrictive environment and its effect on placement of students with intellectual disability. *Inclusion, 4*(2), 56–74. https://doi.org/10.1352/2326-6988-4.2.56

Timothy W. v. Rochester, N. H. School District, 875 F.2d 954 (1st Cir. 1989).

Yell, M. L. (2019). *The law and special education* (5th ed.). Pearson Education.

Yell, M. L., & Prince, A. T. (2022). Why the continuum of alternative placements is essential. In James M. Kauffman (Ed.), *Revitalizing special education* (pp. 59–78). Emerald Publishing Limited.

Chapter Nine

Special Education Teacher Shortage

Most educators enter the teaching profession because of altruistic aspirations to enlighten students and make lasting contributions to society. Education economists, researchers, policy analysts, and leading education figures have concluded that teachers are the most influential in-school factor affecting student success (Hanushek, 2011). All students and especially students with disabilities need **profession-ready** teachers who will prepare them for lives as informed and engaged citizens. Despite the clear need for fully qualified special education teachers, the field has never achieved a fully qualified teaching workforce (Mason-Williams, 2015). Special education teacher shortages are chronic and pervasive within the US public education system. Known as a **supply-and-demand** issue, since the historic passing of the Education for All Handicapped Children Act of 1975 (also known as Public Law 94-142, the precursor to the Individuals with Disabilities Education Act [IDEA, 2004], which mandated that students with disabilities be educated in the public schools), the demand for special education teachers has outpaced the supply (Billingsley & Bettini, 2019). Year after year, almost every state reports a shortage of special education teachers. (US Department of Education, 2023). There are approximately 7.2 million students, or 15% of the total public school enrollment, identified with a disability in K–12 classrooms across the United States (National Center for Education Statistics, 2022). Too many of these students with disabilities are taught by unqualified and underprepared teachers. The complexity and contextual factors of the special education teacher shortage are worth exploring for anyone interested in advocating for students with disabilities. In chapter 9, we will explore the special education teacher shortage and address these essential questions:

1. What are the issues concerning the special education teacher shortage?
2. How do you use the rings of advocacy concerning the special education teacher shortage?
3. Where can I find more information about the special education teacher shortage?

WHAT ARE THE ISSUES CONCERNING THE SPECIAL EDUCATION TEACHER SHORTAGE?

According to the US Bureau of Labor Statistics (2021), there are approximately 470,960 special education teachers in the United States. This number falls short of the current need. The issue is complex but often broken into three areas of need: attracting, preparing, and retaining special educators. We will explain the special education teacher shortage from these three areas of need beginning with the struggle to retain the special education teaching workforce.

Retaining Special Education Teachers

The idea behind **teacher retention** is to keep special educators in the profession and more specifically, to keep great teachers engaged in serving students with disabilities. Despite the appeal of a career in special education, many special education teachers do not stay in the profession for long. According to the US Department of Education's (2012) "Facts about the Teaching Profession," and the National Commission on Teaching and America's Future (2010) founded by the Bill & Melinda Gates Foundation, half of all teachers leave the profession within the first five years, and it is thought that special educators often do not even stay that long (Billingsley & Bettini, 2019). **Teacher attrition** is when special education teachers leave the profession. Many factors including working conditions, preparation and qualifications, job satisfaction, caseload size, student behaviors, administrative supports, and collegial supports significantly influence special education teachers' decisions to stay or leave (Billingsley & Bettini, 2019). Although there is some dispute over accurate teacher attrition rates due to difficulties tracking teachers who leave the profession, move, or take different positions, approximately 16% of all teachers and 25% of special educators leave their positions annually, contributing to the estimated 36,500 vacancies during the 2020–2021 academic year (Carver-Thomas & Darling-Hammond, 2017; Nguyen et al., 2022; IRIS Center, 2013), and these are prepandemic data.

Attracting Special Education Teachers

Teacher attrition alone does not necessitate a shortage. However, teacher attrition is compounded with a nationwide decline in teacher preparation program enrollments as well as a decline in program completion rates (American Association of Colleges for Teacher Education, 2022). Recently, the decline in teacher preparation enrollment has caught the attention of many popular press outlets such as *U.S. News & World Report*, *National Public Radio*, *Education Week*, and *Inside Higher Ed*, all of which speculate how the serious inability to attract new teachers into the profession combined with pandemic-induced teacher burnout has resulted in a "five-alarm crisis" within the education system (e.g., Camera, 2019; Kamenetz, 2022; Knox, 2022; Will, 2022). In response to the snowballing need for a solution, Congress passed the Every Student Succeeds Act (2015), which was intended to remove federal barriers that were negatively affecting teacher recruitment efforts by maximizing state decision-making authority for licensure and credentialing of all teachers including special education teachers. As a result, new pathways to the profession, known as **alternative route programs**, have grown in popularity in the United States. Prospective special education teachers are finding faster pathways into the profession (Connelly et al., 2014; Rosenberg & Sindelar, 2005). These alternative route programs are thought to appeal to nontraditional prospective special educators including individuals from groups that are underrepresented in the teaching workforce (Connelly et al., 2014). From 2019–2020, 30% ($n = 8,610$) of all special education teachers were prepared through alternative route programs (Day, 2022). Critics of this approach to attracting greater numbers into the special education teaching profession point to reduced preparation and licensure standards, or a "lowering of the bar" into the profession. This is where the final piece of this puzzle comes in.

Preparing Special Education Teachers

Yes, many special education teachers are looking for the nearest exit, and new special education teachers are not flooding the front gates. But there is another group we have yet to discuss: current special educators who are unqualified or underprepared to teach students with disabilities. States are filling vacancies with teachers who are not fully credentialed (Peyton et al., 2021). Federal licensure requirements for teachers to be "highly qualified" were eliminated with the enactment of the Every Student Succeeds Act (2015). All decision-making about determining readiness to enter the profession rests with state departments of education. In the absence of the "highly qualified" provision, state departments of education have the flexibility to revise their certification requirements for entry into the profession. This opportunity to simplify the licensure process has resulted in questions about the readiness of special education teachers to successfully do their jobs (Mason-Williams et al., 2020).

While "lowering the bar" may create short-term solutions by ensuring an adult is in every classroom, long-term complications are not clearly addressed. Placing people in classrooms does not necessarily solve the special education teacher shortage. Underprepared or unqualified special education teachers do not stay in the field. Specifically, attrition rates are two to three times higher for teachers who enter the field underprepared (e.g., provisional licensure, emergency licensure, no licensure; Podolsky et al., 2016). Despite the fact that a formal preparation is closely associated with teacher retention (Billingsley & Bettini, 2019; Gilmour & Wehby, 2020), many states have lowered preparation requirements as a short-term teacher shortage solution. For example, Nebraska, California, and Pennsylvania are hiring teacher candidates (i.e., undergraduate students) as long-term substitutes to fill vacant classrooms (Iasevoli, 2018). Oklahoma and Utah are hiring individuals with any college degree and a passing grade on a subject matter exam. New York removed the literacy exam requirement for prospective teachers because too many people were failing it, and Arkansas now allows districts that have requested a waiver of teacher certification to hire anyone with any type of bachelor's degree. In Alabama "adjunct instructors" can teach secondary education with as little as a high school diploma and a clear background check (Klass, 2016). Policy makers, district leaders, and even parents see the genuine need to fill vacant classrooms, but putting individuals who are not prepared to be teachers into teaching positions will not solve the teacher shortage problem and can damage student outcomes given the effect teachers have on student performance (see Carver-Thomas & Darling-Hammond, 2019). Leading researchers in the field have put forth recommendations for these stakeholders in the hopes of making headway with the shortage across research, policy, and practice efforts (see table 9.1).

HOW DO YOU USE THE RINGS OF ADVOCACY CONCERNING THE SPECIAL EDUCATION TEACHER SHORTAGE?

Miss Lazaroni is a special education teacher certified to teach grades one through six. She is in her second year as a special education teacher in a public elementary school. Miss Lazaroni has 20 students from grades two through five on her caseload. She divides up her day by pushing into fourth-grade general education classrooms where her students are learning, teaching fifth-grade reading to the intensive reading group, and pulling out second and

Table 9.1. **Strategies to Mitigate Special Education Teacher Shortages**

Strategy	*Stakeholders*
Support researchers to gather data on teacher shortages.	Policy makers, state education agencies, local education agencies, and school administrators
Prepare leaders to support all teachers and students.	Institutions of higher education
Assess working conditions and tailor remedies to meet the specific needs of schools and districts.	Local education agencies
Provide guidance for assessing attrition and disaggregating workforce data.	State education agencies
Support early career teachers with mentorship opportunities and strong induction support.	Local education agencies and school administrators
Consider differentiating compensation and provide retention incentives.	Policy makers, district leaders, and local education agencies

Adapted from recommendations from Billingsley, B., & Bettini, E. (2019). Special education teacher attrition and retention: A review of the literature. *Review of Educational Research*, 89(5), 697–744. https://doi .org/10.3102/0034654319862495

third grade students for small-group and one-on-one resource room instruction. Miss Lazaroni is feeling very overwhelmed with her new role. It is only her second year after graduating from her preparation program, and now she is taking on teaching second-, third-, fourth-, and fifth-grade students across multiple content areas. Additionally, she has to interact with general education teachers across all of these grade levels but has very little flexibility in her schedule to attend grade-level meetings. Recently, one of the fourth-grade teachers, who took a leave of absence to care for an elderly family member, decided not to return. Miss Lazaroni is familiar with the class because she pushes in during social studies and math to help some of the students on her caseload. The principal asks Miss Lazaroni to cover the fourth-grade class as a substitute since he is having trouble finding consistent coverage for the class. The principal explains he is in a tough position but has to make sure he has an adult in the room to watch the students even if that means the students on Miss Lazaroni's caseload miss out on special education services.

The Problem

Miss Lazaroni knows that the individualized education programs (IEPs) on her caseload will fall out of compliance if she becomes a substitute teacher and cannot provide her students with their legally required special education services. She feels like her students are the recipients of negative, unintended consequences. Miss Lazaroni recognizes that oftentimes in her role, policy decisions are happening to her and are not being made with her. She considers how responses to the special education teacher shortage feel reactive, rather than proactive, and the bottom line is that her students cannot afford to miss out on special education services.

Miss Lazaroni's Solution

Miss Lazaroni's first instinct is to find an immediate solution because she is not ready to take on a long-term substitute position in addition to her current role. She considers that there needs to be both short- and long-term fixes to this problem. Miss Lazaroni is empathetic to the principal's struggles to keep teachers and find reliable substitute teachers, but Miss Lazaroni also knows she has a responsibility to her own caseload of students. She thinks about how she might partner with the other fourth-grade teachers to increase the amount of coverage for this class as well as reviews her own approach to push-in and pull-out services. Miss Lazaroni also plans to reach out to community and family partners to seek long-term solutions.

Rings of Advocacy

Now that Miss Lazaroni has an overall solution to advocate *for*, she needs to identify how to advocate for this solution and whom to advocate *to*. By using the Five Rings of Advocacy Framework (figure 9.1), Miss Lazaroni can organize her advocacy and specifically tailor her efforts across appropriate spheres of influence.

Figure 9.1. The Five Rings of Advocacy

Self-Advocacy Ring

The immediate problem is finding coverage for the vacant fourth-grade class-room. Miss Lazaroni understands this problem, but she knows that she can-not stop providing services to her caseload of students. She considers which stakeholders can be invited to discuss solutions created by this problem. In this scenario, key stakeholders include the reading coach and school leader-ship. Miss Lazaroni reached out to the principal asking for a brainstorming session at the end of the school day. She advocates for herself by explaining other short-term solutions will be necessary because her own caseload of students are relying on her support. She and the principal decide to discuss immediate solutions for the rest of the week. During this brainstorming ses-sion, Miss Lazaroni makes it clear that she wants to help figure out coverage options but she cannot take on additional students onto her already large case-load. While advocating for herself, Miss Lazaroni is intentional about using conversational strategies (e.g., LAFF don't CRY strategy in chapter 3) so that progress is a priority. The principal is open to solutions. They discuss shifting her caseload so that the reading coach takes her fifth-grade reading group for the immediate future. Miss Lazaroni thinks this will ensure the fifth-grade readers are receiving high-quality instruction from the reading coach and she will have an additional 90 minutes each day to help with covering the fourth-grade classroom until a substitute teacher can be identified.

Classroom Advocacy Ring

Miss Lazaroni also proposes a new model of teaching where the students across all three sections of fourth grade rotate through stations during the portions of the day when she has to go meet with other students on her caseload. She considers this a viable option because the students can work through highly structured, small-group and independent activities with less teacher-led instruction. In this model, two teachers can work with multiple **homogeneously grouped** students through rotation. This flexible approach will allow more students in one classroom without increasing the group sizes during direct teacher instruction. The station teaching solution is a large change for all three fourth-grade classrooms because the other two teachers will have 25 more students working in small groups through their rooms for the afternoons. The principal is open to this idea and schedules a meeting with the fourth-grade team for the following school day. He mentions staffing a para-educator in each classroom to support the fourth-grade teachers and their students. Therefore, the para-educators, fourth-grade classroom teach-ers, Miss Lazaroni, and the principal work together to find a viable short-term solution.

School Advocacy Ring

Miss Lazaroni recognizes long-term solutions are also needed. She hears people talk about the important work teachers do in all sorts of social settings such as when she engages in friendly conversation with the local grocery store cashier or chats with others at the dog park. Miss Lazaroni feels strongly that more people might consider a career in education if they realized the serious need for special education teachers in the educator workforce. Miss Lazaroni decides she wants to get the word out to a broader audience about the needs of her school and the field. She decides to start advocating for her school at the monthly parent teacher organizational (PTO) meetings, and she even emails the district fire department and county library to ask if she can speak on behalf of her school. She wants to invite community members to be part of the long-term solution. Miss Lazaroni starts sharing her school's story. She explains they have lost three teachers in the past year and cannot find reliable substitute teachers. She asks people to consider a vocation in teaching.

Miss Lazaroni's emails and meetings with community members pay off. The fire department's lieutenant contacts her to share that his wife is a retired teacher and his sister recently retired after working at the nearby art museum for 25 years. He asks for Miss Lazaroni to share details about how to become a substitute teacher at her school. She replied that she had to learn about the school policies and would be back in touch. She plans to follow up promptly so as not to diminish the momentum she is creating around her cause.

After Miss Lazaroni shares her story with families over coffee and donuts at the PTO meeting, a handful of moms and one dad start to share stories about having lost their jobs during the COVID-19 pandemic. A couple of stay-at-home parents also expressed a desire about returning to school for teaching. They discussed being too old for traditional preparation programs and mentioned that they needed scheduling flexibility and affordability. Miss Lazaroni asks these family members to sign a letter of interest that she planned to share at the school board meeting when she asks for funding to train family and community members to become teachers.

The following month, Miss Lazaroni finally had her chance to present at the school board meeting. She talked about her ideas to get funding for family members to become trained teachers. She also asked that the school board start a campaign modeled after her attempts to connect with community members as potential substitute teachers. She is attacking the problem from multiple angles to identify innovative yet high-probability solutions for her school.

State Advocacy Ring

Miss Lazaroni decides to expand her reach beyond her school since her advocacy efforts seem to be working. She thinks about how other schools might benefit from hearing about her model for activating community members in the long-term fight against the special education teacher shortage. She decides to engage state leaders by making them aware of her successes. Miss Lazaroni drafts a cover letter to her state elected officials and the state secretary of education. She summarizes her efforts and includes the letters of interest from the family members she connected with through the PTO. She wants her state leaders to see the alignment between families and teachers on this issue.

Miss Lazaroni asked the state to consider funding an alternative route program that could allow schools like hers to partner with institutes of higher education and provide family members of students in her school flexibility and funding to become trained teachers. Miss Lazaroni ended her letter with a request for a meeting with her congressperson's office staff. Miss Lazaroni received a call back from the staff person to set up a meeting and discuss these ideas. Apparently, Miss Lazaroni's congressperson has a niece who attends school in the same district who also lost her teacher after last year and thinks involving the community in the solution is an innovative idea.

Federal Advocacy Ring

Miss Lazaroni wants to get involved in advocacy at the federal level. She wants Congress to hear about the successes and struggles of special education teachers like herself. Miss Lazaroni wants the federal government to help with the special education teacher shortage through additional funding for attracting, preparing, and retaining special education teachers. She decides the best way to do this is to seek opportunities for engagement through her national professional organization. Miss Lazaroni is a member of the Council for Exceptional Children (CEC). This is the leading national organization for special education teachers.

As a member of CEC, she always reads the newsletter and community postings on the CEC website. First, she notices a posting about a teacher survey seeking experiences across the country relating to the teacher shortage, and she decides to follow the link and complete the survey. She knows the importance of sharing her voice through special education research. Miss Lazaroni also learned about the Special Education Legislative Summit held each summer where CEC members go to Capitol Hill in D.C. to speak on behalf of the field. She sees mention of funding to cover the costs of member travel through CEC and emails the contact person to ask for an application.

Miss Lazaroni also reaches out to her state chapter of CEC's president and asks for help scheduling meetings with her legislative representatives to discuss her ideas for building up the teaching force within the community to see if there are any federal **flow-through funding streams** that could support these ideas. Plus, Miss Lazaroni plans to ask that they fully fund IDEA in the next **appropriations** bill so more federal dollars go to ensuring all students with disabilities receive the services they are entitled to under the law.

In Conclusion

Miss Lazaroni took the approach of finding a short-term solution while also advocating for long-term change. The special education teacher shortage issue has been a snowballing problem for decades. When it comes to advocating for this issue, we hope the five rings of advocacy (figure 9.1) allow you to compartmentalize various aspects of this complicated problem. As first defined in chapter 2, advocacy is about promoting the interest or cause of someone or a group of people. Within the teacher shortage issue, there are countless variables influenced by contextual factors. Therefore, advocacy can look many different ways. But what is important is to first identify and understand the problem. This includes a thorough examination of local, state, and national circumstances. Next, relevant stakeholders must be invited to the conversation. Although activism draws people's attention to an issue, advocacy is about including people at the table. Finally, solutions are needed to be a successful advocate. We recommend using the five rings of advocacy to serve as a lens for promoting progress and systematically addressing the persistent problem of special education teacher shortages as they relate to your individual situation.

WHERE CAN I FIND MORE INFORMATION ABOUT TEACHER SHORTAGES?

American Association of Colleges for Teacher Education (AACTE) Action Alerts

 Action Alerts are a great way to begin your advocacy at the federal level. AACTE provides intuitive forms to message your congressional representative on a variety of issues related to teacher preparation and teacher shortages. Visit https://aacte .org/policy-and-advocacy/action-alerts/

Journal of Special Education Preparation

The *Journal of Special Education Preparation* is an open-access, peer-reviewed academic journal that provides information and materials related to special education preparation. Articles are written by special education faculty for special education faculty. Take a look at https://openjournals.bsu.edu/JOSEP.

Teacher Education Division, Council for Exceptional Children

The Teacher Education Division (TED) of the CEC is a division of the CEC devoted exclusively to issues affecting the preparation of special education practitioners, including teacher shortages. Explore it at https://tedcec.org/.

Teacher Education and Special Education

Teacher Education and Special Education is an academic journal that publishes research articles related to the preparation and professional development of teachers, scholars, leaders, and other support personnel who work with students with disabilities. Visit https://journals.sagepub.com/home/tes.

KEY TERMS

alternative route programs: Pathways to gain state licensure that typically bypass traditional teacher certification requirements.

appropriations: A legal authorization to make specified expenditures for specified purposes.

flow-through funding streams: Grant programs that allocate money based on formulas set by Congress.

homogeneously grouped: Grouping students based on similar academic abilities.

profession ready: A teacher who has demonstrated the skills and knowledge needed for effective classroom practice prior to licensure.

supply and demand: Production of enough teachers to meet the needs of the field.

teacher attrition: The percentage of teachers exiting the educational profession each year.

teacher retention: The percentage of teachers who remain teaching in the same school from year to year.

DISCUSSION QUESTIONS

1. What are your experiences with teacher shortages?
2. How would you use the five rings of advocacy if you were in Miss Lazaroni's position?
3. How can best practices in attracting, retaining, and preparing special education teachers affect the teacher shortage crisis?
4. What are some obstacles to addressing the teacher shortage issue?
5. Discuss the issues around traditional teacher preparation programs versus alternative route programs and the need for profession-ready teachers.

REFERENCES

American Association of Colleges for Teacher Education. (2022, March). *Colleges of education: A national portrait* (2nd ed.)*.* https://www.aacteconnect360.org/viewdocument/colleges-of-education-a-national-p-1

Billingsley, B., & Bettini, E. (2019). Special education teacher attrition and retention: A review of the literature. *Review of Educational Research, 89*(5), 697–744. https://doi.org/10.3102/0034654319862495

Camera, L. (2019, March). Sharp nationwide enrollment drop in teacher prep programs cause for alarm. *U.S. News & World Report.* https://www.usnews.com/news/education-news/articles/2019-12-03/sharp-nationwide-enrollment-drop-in-teacher-prep-programs-cause-for-alarm

Carver-Thomas D., & Darling-Hammond, L. (2017). *Teacher turnover: Why it matters and what we can do about it.* Learning Policy Institute.

Carver-Thomas, D., & Darling-Hammond, L. (2019). The trouble with teacher turnover: How teacher attrition affects students and schools. *Education Policy Analysis Archives, 27*(36). http://dx.doi.org/10.14507/epaa.27.3699

Connelly, V. J., Rosenberg, M. S., & Larson, K. E. (2014). Alternative routes for special education teacher preparation: Context, outcomes, and implications. In P. T. Sindelar, E. McCray, M. T. Brownell, and B. Lignagaris/Kraft (Eds), *Handbook of research on special education teacher preparation* (pp. 215–230). Routledge.

Day, J. (2022). *Alternative route programs and special education teacher preparation* [Unpublished dissertation]. George Mason University.

Every Student Succeeds Act of 2015, Pub. L. No. 114-95 § 4104.

Gilmour, A. F., & Wehby, J. H. (2020). The association between teaching students with disabilities and teacher turnover. *Journal of Educational Psychology, 112*(5), 1042–1060. https://doi.org/10.1037/edu0000394

Hanushek, E. A. (2011). The economic value of higher teacher quality. *Economics of Education Review, 30*(3), 466–479. https://doi.org/10.1016/j.econedurev.2010.12.006

Iasevoli, B. (2018, April). Can hiring ed. school students help solve substitute teacher shortages? *Education Week.* http://blogs.edweek.org/edweek/teacherbeat/2018/04/can_hiring_ed_school_students_solve_substitute_teacher_shortages.html

IRIS Center. (2013). *Teacher retention: Reducing the attrition of special educators.* https://iris.peabody.vanderbilt.edu/module/tchr-ret/

Kamenetz, A. (2022, February). More than half of teachers are looking for the exits, a poll says. *NPR.* https://www.npr.org/2022/02/01/1076943883/teachers-quitting-burnout

Klass, K. (2016, January). State allows non-certified teachers in classroom. *Montgomery Advertiser.* https://www.montgomeryadvertiser.com/story/news/2016/01/28/state-allows-non-certified-teachers-classroom/79466980/

Knox, L. (2022, August 29). Teacher education programs desperately seek students. *Inside Higher Ed.* https://www.insidehighered.com/news/2022/08/29/teacher-shortage-tied-education-programs-enrollment-drop#:~:text=Between%20 2008%20and%202019%2C%20the,of%20Colleges%20for%20Teacher%20 Education

Mason-Williams, L. (2015). Unequal opportunities: A profile of the distribution of special education teachers. *Exceptional Children, 81*(2), 247–262. https://doi.org/10.1177/0014402914551737

Mason-Williams, L., Bettini, E., Peyton, D., Harvey, A., Rosenberg, M., & Sindelar, P. T. (2020). Rethinking shortages in special education: Making good on the promise of an equal opportunity for students with disabilities. *Teacher Education and Special Education, 43*(1), 45–62. https://doi.org/10.1177/0888406419880352

National Center for Educational Statistics. (2022, May). *Students with disabilities.* https://nces.ed.gov/programs/coe/indicator/cgg/students-with-disabilities

National Commission on Teaching and America's Future. (2010, January). *Who will teach? Experience matters.* https://files.eric.ed.gov/fulltext/ED511985.pdf

Nguyen, T. D., Lam, C. B., & Bruno, P. (2022). *Is there a national teacher shortage? A systematic examination of reports of teacher shortages in the United States.* (EdWorkingPaper: 22-631). Annenberg Institute at Brown University.

Peyton, D. J., Acosta, K., Harvey, A., Pua, D. J., Sindelar, P. T., Mason-Williams, L., . . . Crews, E. (2021). Special education teacher shortage: Differences between high and low shortage states. *Teacher Education and Special Education, 44*(1), 5–23. https://doi.org/10.1177/0888406420906618

Podolsky, A., Kini, T., Bishop, J., & Darling-Hammond, L. (2016). *Solving the teacher shortage: How to attract and retain excellent educators.* Learning Policy Institute.

Rosenberg, M., & Sindelar, P. T. (2005). The proliferation of alternative routes to certification in special education: A critical review of the literature. *Journal of Special Education, 39*(2), 117–127. https://doi.org/10.1177/00224669050390020201

US Bureau of Labor Statistics. (2021, May). *Occupational employment and wage statistics.* https://www.bls.gov/oes/current/oes_nat.htm#25-0000

US Department of Education. (2012). *Facts about the teaching profession for a national conversation about teaching.* https://www2.ed.gov/documents/respect/teaching-profession-facts.doc

US Department of Education. (2023). *Teacher shortage areas.* https://tsa.ed.gov/#/
    reports

Will, M. (2022, March). Fewer people are getting teacher degrees. Prep programs
    sound the alarm. *Education Week.* https://www.edweek.org/teaching-learning/
    fewer-people-are-getting-teacher-degrees-prep-programs-sound-the-alarm/2022/03

Chapter Ten

Inequities in Special Education

Advocating effectively to politicians, bureaucrats, and school leaders is essential to making meaningful change in our classrooms, schools, and communities. Although a detailed understanding of *how* to advocate across the different rings is critical and something we hope you gained in other chapters in this book, understanding the issues and arguments for which people are actively advocating for and against is equally essential. If you have read chapters 8 and 9, you have a well-rounded understanding of two major issues in special education: the debate surrounding inclusion and the effect of special education teacher shortages. These two topics are closely associated with equity issues; however, other important inequities can and have prompted widespread advocacy. As a novice or expert advocate in the field of special education, these are issues that may arise frequently, and as such, they should be familiar to you.

In this final chapter, we will explain inequities in special education that have prompted a high degree of advocacy and robust debate across the five rings of advocacy (figure 10.1). It is not our intention to explain every facet of these complex issues. Instead, we intend to give you an overview of the issue, the most up-to-date research, and a description of different perspectives. As you read, recall what you have learned from previous chapters, consider how these issues span the rings of advocacy, acknowledge the ring from which you may advocate, and contemplate how you might apply your advocacy skills to remedy these inequities. In doing so, we will explore the topic of inequities in special education and answer these essential questions:

1. What are some issues concerning inequities in special education?
2. How do you use the rings of advocacy concerning issues of equity?
3. Where can I find more information about inequities in special education?

State Advocacy

Classroom Advocacy

Self Advocacy

School Advocacy

Federal Advocacy

Figure 10.1. The Five Rings of Advocacy

WHAT ARE SOME ISSUES CONCERNING INEQUITIES IN SPECIAL EDUCATION?

Before any discussion is had about inequities in special education, an important distinction must be made between two terms: **inequity** and **inequality**. Both terms center around the concept of resource allocation (e.g., time, opportunity, money); however, the distinction is important. Inequality refers to an unequal allocation of resources, meaning there is an imbalance in the sameness of distribution. Equality promotes fairness and justice by giving everyone the same amount of resources. There is no consideration about the amount of resources one starts with. For example, two students are in a classroom, and both students receive 10 minutes of the teacher's support. That is an equal distribution of teacher time.

Inequity considers contextual factors of a situation and acknowledges that resource allocation depends on individual needs. In other words, equity is about fairness and justice by making sure everyone has access to the same opportunities. Considering the previous example, let's say one student is proficient in the lesson content and is completing the individual assignment with no problem. The other student is not yet proficient and is needing extra help. Although both students received an equal amount of teacher support (i.e., 10 minutes), that is not an equitable distribution of support because one student needs additional support to succeed like their peer. Equity is about remedying an imbalance by providing more of the resource to those who begin with less or require more due to circumstances. Students with disabilities often require more individualized support to make adequate educational progress compared to their nondisabled peers. While disabled and nondisabled students may receive an unequal amount of a given service (e.g., personalized one-to-one attention, access to accommodations, modified assignments), educational opportunity is equitable if those in need of additional service are afforded such services. Although some may use the terms educational inequality and inequity interchangeably, one should understand a distinct difference between the two.

Recognizing education inequities is a crucial precursor to remedying them. Upon careful inspection, you may find inequities in your state, district, school, or classroom. One strategy for recognizing inequities involves identifying factors outside a particular student or group of students that is creating an undue advantage or disadvantage. Although a primary goal of public education and special education is equal access to educational opportunity, factors such as historical and systemic barriers, geographic location, socioeconomic status, adverse childhood experiences, and of course, disability status have limited the ability of students to have the same access to high-quality education. Despite the efforts of advocates throughout history and even today, inequities still exist and require a new generation of well-informed, skillful, and persistent advocates to both recognize inequities and apply their advocacy skills for change.

In the following section, we discuss inequity issues that you may hear about in the field of special education. This is not intended to be an exhaustive list. In fact, now that you have been learning to identify and understand problems, you will likely find context-specific inequities in your preparation programs, schools, or classrooms.

Disproportionality

Disproportionality in special education most commonly refers to the overrepresentation or underrepresentation of groups of students in contrast to their share of the general population (Kauffman et al., 2017). Special education stakeholders often note the overrepresentation of minority students receiving special education services due to their race or ethnicity (Anastasiou et al., 2017). Similarly, disproportionality can refer to the overrepresentation of minority students in a more restrictive environment or disproportionate punishment for minority students (National Center for Learning Disabilities, 2017). The term *minority students* may appear inclusive, yet with regard to disproportionality, it typically refers to students in the following racial or ethnic groups: Black/African American, Hispanic/Latinx students, and American Indian/Alaska Native.

Despite a recent policy push to explore disparities, the extent to which minority students are overrepresented in special education is not fully known. Under the Individuals with Disabilities Education Act (IDEA, 2004) Part B, states must report significant racial disproportionality concerning the identification and placement of students with disabilities. States are also required to report racial disproportionality regarding disciplinary action, including the duration and type of action taken. According to the US Department of Education (2022), "The standard methodology uses risk ratios to analyze disparities for seven racial or ethnic groups, comparing each to all other children within the local education agency (LEA) in 14 different categories of analysis. States determine the thresholds above which the risk ratio in each category of analysis indicates significant disproportionality" (para. 2).

In their report to Congress on the implementation of IDEA, the US Department of Education (2021) noted that racial disparities do exist concerning the identification and placement of students. Specifically, based on 2019 data, African American/Black, Hispanic/Latinx, and Native American students were more likely to be identified for special education services than their White or Asian peers. Regarding placement, most students in each racial category were educated in the general education setting for at least 80% or more of the day. Still, Asian, Native Hawaiian, Black/African American, and Hispanic/Latinx students with disabilities spent the least percentage of their instructional time in the general education setting.

Studies from research organizations and universities have found similar disparities, and their findings highlight potential reasons for such disparities, particularly in identification. Bal and colleagues (2014) found that the risk for overidentification was highest for students who were African American, American Indian, receiving free or reduced lunch, and male. Anderson and colleagues (2015) found that boys were 2.29 times more likely to be identified as a student with disabilities between kindergarten and fourth grade than girls.

Researchers have also identified that the relationship between **socioeconomic status** (SES) and special education identification is significant, meaning SES may influence special education identification (Zhang et al., 2014). In their longitudinal study, Zhang and colleagues found that female students from families with high SES and higher expectations for postsecondary education were less likely to be identified as needing special education services between kindergarten and fourth grade than other groups. In addition, higher parental expectations were associated with lower special education identification rates.

There is, however, some research that counters common conceptions about disproportionality. A nationally representative study found that students from racial or ethnic groups with similar exposure to poverty, gender, and English learner status were consistently less likely than White children to be identified as having a disability (Morgan et al., 2017).

The mixed nature of research on the prevalence and uncertain contributors of overrepresentation makes disproportionality one of many hot-button issues in the field. Anastasiou and colleagues (2017) explain that disproportionality has been viewed as controversial for at least four reasons (1) disproportionate representation in special education is believed to constitute another example of systemic racial bias in the United States, (2) it is believed that labeling students as intellectually disabled or emotionally disabled may carry a negative societal stigma, (3) the discussion of disproportionality leads to questions of the effectiveness of special education in general, and (4) disproportionality is closely related to other forms of **identity politics**, which can be controversial and easily politicized.

Identity politics refers to political theory and activism geared at representing specific groups of people based on facets of their identity, such as race, ethnicity, religion, sexual orientation, and other characteristics (Bernstein, 2005). In fact, one of the first uses of the term was by Anspach (1979), who used it to refer to disability rights advocates attempting to change the public perception of people living with disabilities. In recent years, identity politics has gained numerous critics and an increasingly negative connotation, particularly in the political sphere. Critics argue that rather than coalition building, identity politics results in insular and exclusive groups that focus on divisive issues (Tarrow, 1998). Even so, the foundation of modern identity politics is primarily rooted in the civil rights movements of the 1960s and 1970s and has served to organize support for various issues, including disability rights and special education.

Exclusionary Discipline and Restraint and Seclusion

Another issue regarding equity in special education that directly affects many students, teachers, and administrators is discipline. Disproportionate discipline for minoritized students is one facet of the disproportionality discussion. Researchers have found that minoritized students have disproportionately higher suspension rates compared to other groups (Zhang et al., 2004). Similarly, disparities in suspension rates exist between geographic areas. For example, students in the western states were more likely to be removed by school personnel than students in other geographic regions. Issues surrounding discipline processes for students with disabilities exist in the field and extend beyond discrepancies based on race, ethnicity, and geographic region. Two prominent issues include exclusionary discipline for students with disabilities and restraint and seclusion.

Gordon (2018) explains that quantifying discrimination is a major challenge because "researchers essentially attempt to exhaust all other plausible explanations for observed gaps in outcomes across whatever groups are involved" (para. 9). She explains that disproportionate discipline is tough to identify because researchers do not observe the behavior of concern but rather the infraction as described by the school or administration. Bias, whether unconscious or deliberate, could play a role in determining whether an infraction occurred. Skiba and colleagues (2011) found that Black and Hispanic/Latinx students were significantly more likely than their White peers to be referred for disciplinary action. Additionally, minority students were more likely to receive expulsion or out-of-school suspension for behaviors similar or identical to those exhibited by their White peers. Barrett and colleagues (2017) found similar results, noting that Black students and students from low SES backgrounds are disciplined more often than other students across districts and schools. When considering discipline history and background characteristics, Black students receive longer suspensions after participating in interracial physical altercations (Barrett et al., 2017).

Disproportionate discipline extends to students with disabilities as well as students with intersecting identities. **Intersectionality** refers to how the overlapping facets of our identities (e.g., race, ethnicity, gender, sexual orientation, disability status) intersect to create unique and dynamic effects and experiences (Crenshaw, 2018). Sullivan and colleagues (2014) found that disability type, gender, race/ethnicity, and family SES were significant predictors of suspension among students with disabilities. Students with emotional and behavioral disorders were at increased risk for suspension. It is important to note that students' disability status is only one facet of their identities. Other attributes such as race, SES, and English proficiency status can intersect with disability status to create unique experiences. For example, a student who is an English language learner with a learning disability may have very different academic and functional outcomes than a student from a high SES family with a learning disability.

Researchers and others have hypothesized that disproportionate discipline for minority students and students with disabilities is at least in part due to **implicit bias**. Implicit bias refers to the attitudes or stereotypes we assign to people without conscious knowledge. Examples of implicit bias, as well as its effect, are far reaching. For example, perhaps a teacher wrongly assumes a student has a happy home life because they come from a family with a high SES. As a result, that teacher attributes the student's pompous and disrespectful behavior to a sense of entitlement rather than its actual cause: a coping mechanism for their parents' combative relationship. Perhaps an administrator may subconsciously assume that a minority student is a "bad kid" after being caught vaping in the bathroom and suspends the student but overlooks the same behavior when done by a White student. Recognizing our implicit biases is a key precursor to implementing equitable practices and advocating for meaningful change.

Another inequitable practice in special education is the use of **restraint** and **seclusion** for students with disabilities. Restraint of a student refers to "restricting the student's ability to move his or her torso, arms, legs or head freely" (US Department of Education, 2016, p. 2). Seclusion of a student refers to "confining a student alone in a room or area he or she is not permitted to leave" (US Department of Education, 2016, p. 2). In their most recent and extensive guidance on this issue, the US Department of Education (2012) provided guidelines for the use of restraint and seclusion, noting,

> Restraint or seclusion should not be used as routine school safety measures; that is, they should not be implemented except in situations where a child's behavior poses imminent danger of serious physical harm to self or others and not as a routine strategy implemented to address instructional problems or inappropriate behavior (e.g., disrespect, noncompliance, insubordination, out of seat), as a means of coercion or retaliation, or as a convenience. (p. 3)

Gage and colleagues (2020) found that students with disabilities were seven times more likely to be restrained and four times more likely to be secluded than their peers without disabilities. Given limits to individual freedom and risk of injury brought about by restraint and seclusion paired with the need to ensure student safety, there are differing viewpoints on the value of restraint and seclusion. Although most agree that restraint and seclusion should be rare and only used to protect student safety, there has been a movement to severely limit the instances where restraint or seclusion is acceptable. Distinctions between the types of restraint also inform the discussion regarding this issue. Chemical restraint refers to using unprescribed or inappropriately administered medication to sedate students, control behavior, or restrict freedom. Mechanical restraint involves devices to limit a student's freedom of movement. Finally, physical restraint is a personal restriction of a student's freedom of movement. Though not yet passed into law, the Keeping All Students Safe Act (2021) was introduced in the 117th Congress. It sought to outlaw seclusion, mechanical restraint, and chemical restraint in all schools. If passed, it would encourage strategies to limit the use of physical restraint. Ways of limiting instances of physical restraint include training in de-escalation and trauma-informed practices and implementing Positive Behavior Interventions and Supports (PBIS) programs.

Pandemic-Related Learning Loss

Disproportionality in identification, placement, and discipline and the debate over restraint and seclusion have been ongoing subjects of advocacy and research for over a decade. In contrast, the onset of the COVID-19 pandemic was sudden and traumatic, yet the effects will linger for years. Beyond the immediate public health concerns, several challenges arose from the pandemic, including concerns about increasing rates of childhood anxiety and depression, fierce debates over in-person and virtual learning, and the inability to provide services for students with disabilities. One long-standing problem affecting districts, schools, teachers, families, and students is the continued need to cope with pandemic-related **learning loss**.

Using data from the Nation's Report Card, the Education Recovery Scorecard (2022) reported that due to the COVID-19 pandemic, public school students in the United States lost, on average, a half year of learning in math and a quarter of a year in reading. Six percent of US public school students were in a school that lost more than a year of learning in math. Further, the authors note, "The pandemic widened disparities in achievement between high and low poverty schools. The quarter of schools with the highest shares of students receiving federal lunch subsidies missed two-thirds of a year of math learning, while the quarter of schools with the fewest low-income students lost two-fifths of a year" (para. 6). Although the achievement disparities between high- and low-income districts are alarming, the effect of pandemic-related learning loss for students with disabilities is particularly concerning due to a lack of available data.

After reviewing hundreds of studies examining the effects of the pandemic on student achievement, Stelitano and colleagues (2022) found that less than one-third of studies regarding pandemic-related learning loss disaggregated their data to include disability status. The few studies that explicitly mentioned students with disabilities noted an extensive list of concerns. First, as students returned to in-person instruction, more students with disabilities were identified as having mental health challenges, including anxiety and depression. More children, mainly aged birth to two, were at risk of not being identified for services, and students' transition services and progress toward graduation were seriously disrupted. Stelitano and colleagues (2022) also found that districts have increased their reliance on underqualified teachers, further degrading the quality of the teacher workforce and thereby making learning recovery an even more significant challenge.

There is a timely need for advocacy in learning recovery for students with disabilities. Given long-standing teacher shortages in special education (see chapter 9), recovery from this widespread disruption will be a long-term challenge for states, districts, schools, teachers, families, and students with disabilities. Looking at this systemic issue through an equity lens is helpful for advocates who may be unsure where to begin their work.

HOW DO YOU USE THE RINGS OF ADVOCACY CONCERNING ISSUES OF EQUITY?

Miss Jackson is a high school special education teacher in a large suburban school that serves over 2,000 students. She went through an alternate certification program and has worked as a teacher with a provisional license for three years. She is excited because at the end of this school year, she will finish her preparation program and obtain her professional license and master's degree in special education. Given the effect of COVID during her first two years, many teachers at the school have explained that this is the first year in some time that has "felt somewhat normal." Miss Jackson, too, finally feels a sense of normalcy and routine, though her workday and school is not without challenges. She feels like she can reliably perform many of her responsibilities, although district-wide changes have brought about some new challenges.

Given that the courses she teaches span two subjects and two grade levels, Miss Jackson has a strong network of colleagues and co-teachers across the school. In addition to teaching history and English in the general education setting, she also teaches a study skills class. Through her three years at Lakeside High, she has taught multiple subjects across all four grade levels. Based on this experience, Miss Jackson has gotten to know the strengths and needs of a wide range of students and has experienced firsthand changing student demographics.

At the beginning of Miss Jackson's first year at Lakeside High, the Fairfield County Public Schools changed their school boundaries. Though many consider Fairfield County a relatively affluent suburb of a major metropolitan city, there are significant pockets of poverty and a large population of undocumented immigrants. In fact, Fairfield County has one of the highest measures of income inequality in the country. Although many families have dual incomes and live in million-dollar homes, others often share one-bedroom apartments with one or two other families. Before the boundary change, many students from lower-income families attended a different high school. The school board, to be more equitable with district resources, decided to shift the school boundaries to bring students from more low SES families into Lakeside High. This decision brought about controversy in the community. It spurred protests from more financially affluent community members who worried that the anticipated need for more support for the new students would disrupt the desirable status quo for the existing student body and degrade the schools' exceptional reputation. A staunch proponent for equitable practices for all students, Miss Jackson, who lives in the community, was disheartened by this debate. However, being a new teacher and a county employee at the time, she thought it was best to remain silent and impartial to the contentious debate.

The Problem

For Miss Jackson, the debate from three years ago surrounding the attendance of low-income students at Lakeside High School prompted a desire to advocate for equitable practices. During her first year of teaching, the population of Lakeside High School was 70% White, 11% Asian/Pacific Islander, 9% Hispanic/Latinx, 5% Black/African American, and 5% other racial/ethnic identities. This year, the racial and ethnic demographics are significantly different. Fifty percent of the students identify as White, 30% as Hispanic/Latinx, 8% as other racial/ethnic identities, 7% as Black, and 5% as Asian/Pacific Islander. During her first year, 27% of students at Lakeside received free and reduced lunch. These children live in families with incomes below 130% of the poverty level or receive subsidized food benefits. Today, 53% of the students at Lakeside receive free and reduced lunch. Students with disabilities used to account for 13% of the total student body. Today, 22% of students at Lakeside High School receive special education services.

Miss Jackson's caseload has grown from 20 to 30 in just three years. Although her preparation has allowed her to "keep her head above water," she and her colleagues have had to adjust to the new needs of the students at the school. One concerning pattern that Miss Jackson has noted is an increased number of discipline referrals. Although Miss Jackson has not referred any students to the administration for disciplinary action, she has heard from other teachers around the school that the behavior of "some students" is "completely unacceptable." They claim that vandalism, marijuana use, and fighting are "through the roof." Being a relatively new teacher whose first year was primarily taught online, Miss Jackson does not have a reference point for normal levels of discipline referrals. She is unsure if the talk of an increased number of referrals is a result of poor classroom management, behavior regression due to a year of online learning, implicit bias toward the new population of students, or something else entirely.

Miss Jackson has an interesting conversation with some of her students during her self-contained study skills class. The class is small, consisting of 10 students, two of whom are girls. All but one of the students are students of color. Seven receive free and reduced lunch, and three receive both special education and English language learner services. As they enter the classroom, Miss Jackson asks them how their day went. One of the students, Devon, explains that he is doing "horribly" because a teacher wrote a discipline referral for insubordination. He explains the situation as other students listen in. As Devon finishes his story, other students in the class share similar experiences. They explain that they have been sent to the office for being tardy, violating the dress code, and using inappropriate language. One of the students said a teacher asked him if he was in a gang because he was wearing a blue shirt. Another student chimes in and announces, "They don't ask the White kids questions like that!" Miss Jackson remains quiet for a moment. She does not know what to say but listens quietly as the students continue to share their concerns. Clearly, issues involving behavior and discipline are a challenge for many of the teachers and the students at Lakeside High. She wonders if there is a solution and how she might advocate for it.

Miss Jackson's Solution

During her teacher preparation program, Miss Jackson took a behavior intervention course. One of the classes in that course centered on disproportionate discipline for minority students with disabilities. For one of her assignments, she read Green and colleagues (2019) who explained strategies to address disproportionate exclusionary discipline practices at the school level. Three recommendations included forming a school-wide **equity team**, supporting evidence-based decision-making and using disaggregated discipline data. Miss Jackson decides to follow this plan. She begins by considering the possibility of creating a school-wide equity team. An equity team is a group of individuals representing various educational stakeholders at a school. "The purpose of the team is to create and maintain systems that have an explicit commitment to equity and distinct plans for routinely analyzing disaggregated data, problem-solving, and monitoring the effectiveness of action plans and current systems" (Green et al., 2019, p. 243; figure 10.2).

Rings of Advocacy

Now that Miss Jackson has an overall solution to advocate *for*, she needs to identify how to advocate for this solution and whom to advocate *to*. By using the five rings of advocacy framework (figure 10.1), Miss Jackson can organize her advocacy and specifically tailor her efforts across appropriate spheres of influence.

Self-Advocacy Ring

Miss Jackson knows the first step to effective advocacy is identifying and understanding a problem. Miss Jackson is concerned because she knows that

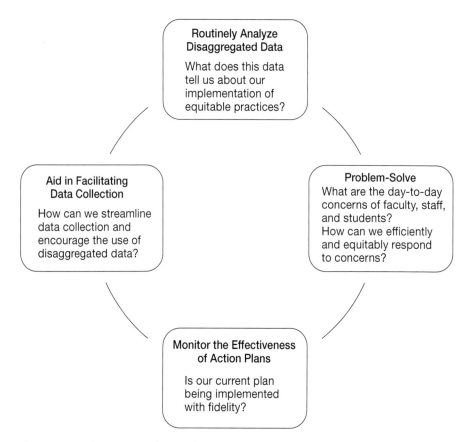

Figure 10.2. The Purpose of an Equity Team

Note. Adapted from Addressing and preventing disproportionality in exclusionary discipline practices for students of color with disabilities," by A. L. Green, D. R. Cohen, and M. Stormont, 2019, *Intervention in School and Clinic*, 54(4), pp. 241–245 (https://doi.org/10.1177/1053451218782437).

the issue of disproportionate discipline for students of color is an issue that is closely intertwined with issues of race, poverty, ableism, and implicit bias. These issues are closely related to the concept of **privilege**. Privilege can take many forms, including privileges of race, gender, sexual orientation, immigration status, and geographic location—just to name a few. The presence of privilege or lack thereof can also spur contentious debates, quickly leading to heightened emotions. As she considers how to begin forming the equity team, Miss Jackson commits to recognizing her own privilege and accepting the identities of all members of her school community.

Self-advocacy is advocating for one's own interests. Although it may seem tactless to say so, Miss Jackson has a vested interest in limiting the instances of exclusionary discipline for students of color at Lakeside High. Miss Jackson understands that exclusionary discipline results in problems for both students and teachers. Exclusionary discipline, such as suspensions, result in lost instructional time. If Miss Jackson's students are suspended and unavailable for learning, they will require additional support to be brought up to speed with the rest of the class. This will add additional responsibilities to her already extensive workload. Furthermore, exclusionary discipline, particularly for students with disabilities, results in a great deal of paperwork and other procedural measures, which shortens Miss Jackson's time to plan and implement instruction. As she seeks to gather stakeholders, allies, and overall buy-in, Miss Jackson highlights that limiting the instances of exclusionary discipline across the school will increase teachers' workload manageability. Not only will this make the school a more equitable place, but it will also allow teachers to spend their limited time better meeting students' academic and functional needs.

Classroom Advocacy Ring

Miss Jackson strives for a welcoming and safe classroom for all students. Based on the conversation from her small-group class, she understands that many of her students do not feel respected or comfortable at Lakeside High. As a result, she is sure to remind the students that every student is respected and valued in her class. Miss Jackson thanks her students for sharing their concerns and briefly explains her proposal for changes. In student-friendly language, Miss Jackson shares that school leaders know disproportionate discipline is an issue and are working collaboratively to find and implement solutions. Miss Jackson also communicates the message to the families of students on her caseload and makes herself available to answer any questions.

Miss Jackson understands that managing student behaviors has been a challenge for some teachers at her school, including many general education teachers. She shares Green and colleagues' (2019) recommendations with her co-teachers and other general education teachers. She wants to encourage and facilitate open and honest communication regarding student discipline with her many co-teachers to ensure that they share similar expectations. She also explains that students' exclusion from the classroom may contribute to student learning loss, which is another pressing issue at Lakeside High. All of her co-teachers are eager to "try anything." They tell her that she may have suggestions that they have not yet considered, and they agree to gauge interest in her school-wide equity team with their general education colleagues.

School Advocacy Ring

Miss Jackson understands that this school-wide problem requires a comprehensive school-wide solution and collaboration with many different
stakeholders. As a well-respected figure at the school, she talks with some
colleagues who share her commitment to equity. Given that it was her idea
to form this team, she asks for her administrator's approval and agrees to
lead the team. Her administrator, who expresses a commitment to improving
discipline procedures, is thrilled that Miss Jackson is willing to take on this
added responsibility. She gives Miss Jackson her support, and with that, Miss
Jackson has a crucial ally.

The team sets out to follow the recommendations of Green and colleagues
(2019). The equity team and school administrators understand that recent
changes in the school's demographics have introduced new challenges.
Namely, students have needs that many teachers are unprepared to meet. With
the support of school administrators, the equity team proposes and prepares
a series of school-wide professional development activities centering on **cultural competence** and **culturally responsive teaching**. Cultural competence
refers to the ability to understand, appreciate, and interact with individuals
from other cultures. Similarly, culturally responsive teaching refers to a pedagogy that incorporates students' customs, perspectives, characteristics, and
lived experiences to improve instruction and encourage students of color to
see themselves as valued in academic spaces.

The equity team decides to gather disaggregated data on the number of
discipline referrals. This often takes the form of noting the identities of
members of the overall population. At Miss Jackson's suggestion, the equity
team asks all teachers at Lakeside High to document any and all referrals
to the administration in a form. Based on the recommendations of McIntosh and colleagues (2014) and Green and colleagues (2019), the form asks
teachers to list the student's name, problem behavior, location, time of day,
type of consequence, and race/ethnicity (table 10.1). Miss Jackson knows
this level of detail will allow the equity team and administrators to identify patterns and determine the extent to which students of color are being
referred at greater rates than their White peers. Miss Jackson and the equity
team facilitate the data collection for one month with her administrator's
assistance.

After one month, a better picture of the prevalence and extent of the problem is available. Based on the disaggregated data, it does appear that students
of color at Lakeside High are being subjected to more instances of exclusionary discipline than their White peers. The equity team meets to discuss potential solutions and how they will advocate to their administrator for policy

Table 10.1. Disaggregated Discipline Referral

Student Name		Student Grade	
Referring staff		Date	
Location		Time	
Race/ethnicity		Disability status	

Problem Behavior	*Possible Motivation*
• Inappropriate language • Physical contact • Defiance • Disrespect • Noncompliance • Disruption • Property misuse • Stealing • Lying • Tardy • Other:	• Obtain peer attention • Obtain adult attention • Obtain items • Avoid peers • Avoid adults • Avoid task or activity • Don't know • Other:

Intervention/Consequence	
• Restate expectation • Re-teach expectation • Use positive reinforcement • Ignore • Use social skills instruction • Use proximity control • Remove problem item • Have student conference • Change seating arrangement • Reward alternate behavior • Redirect • Provide choices	• Initiate classroom behavior plan • Require break outside classroom • Use individual behavior checklist • Use individual behavior plan • Adjust assignments • Reward alternative behavior • Remove reinforcement • Reinforce peers • Contact family • Have family conference • Refer to behavior support team • Refer to office

Time Away from Learning If the student left the classroom, approximately how many minutes were they away?	_____ minutes
Teacher's Description of Events Please briefly describe what prompted this referral	

Comments

changes. One of the equity team members mentions an article she read by the National Association for Secondary School Principals (2020). After reviewing the data, the authors encourage equity team members and administrators to (a) analyze current policies to understand how specific groups are marginalize; (b) provide cultural competency professional development for faculty and staff to better understand how to work with students and their families; (c) identify specific individuals to organize data and manage student progress consistently; and (d) ensure staff members, students, and families understand the purpose of the policy changes and commit to following the program with fidelity. Miss Jackson and the equity team decide that this course of action is the best strategy for making positive changes in their school.

State Advocacy Ring

Miss Jackson recognizes that the challenge of disproportionate discipline is not isolated to Lakeside High School. Based on her research on the state board of education website and recent reports in the local media, she understands that schools across her state have experienced shifting student demographics and similar issues of equity resulting from underprepared educators. In a search for stakeholders, she writes her local state representative and the state department of education. She knows that state education agencies (SEAs) are responsible for teacher licensure requirements.

Given the effectiveness of Lakeside's professional development and the strong research base supporting culturally responsive teaching, she wonders if she can encourage the SEAs to incorporate a class regarding cultural competence into state licensure requirements for new teachers. She writes a professional letter to both her state representative and the SEAs. In her letter, she shares the success at Lakeside High, succinctly describes the research supporting culturally responsive teaching, and describes the feasibility of her ask. Miss Jackson knows that there is power in numbers, so she brings a copy of her letter to a meeting of the equity team. She encourages team members to write their state representatives and the SEAs. To increase her outreach, she also becomes an active member in her state unit of the Council for Exceptional Children (CEC). There, she hopes to advocate for more instruction in culturally responsive teaching across the state. She networks with colleagues across the state, shares the progress at Lakeside, and asks questions to explore what specific policies have been effective for their schools and communities.

Federal Advocacy Ring

Although Miss Jackson is initially apprehensive about advocating at the federal ring, she knows there is a need to take her advocacy to the highest level. In fact, one of her colleagues at the state division of CEC shared an article by Gordon (2018) that outlines the national issue of disproportionality in exclusionary discipline. She brainstorms with members of the state unit, and they encourage her to participate in the Special Education Legislative Summit, where she can advocate for the needs of her students in her district and their state at the federal level.

She connects with members of CEC's Special Education Legislative Summit team, and they share more information with her. Miss Jackson eagerly agrees to attend this advocacy event, which is held in Washington, D.C., every summer. There, she feels well supported and prepared to make her ask. Her meetings with congressional staff go better than expected. Prefacing the conversation with her role as a teacher, advocate, and constituent, she explains the positive changes she has seen at Lakeside High, her work encouraging licensure changes, and her hopes for the passage of a law like the Keeping All Students Safe Act (2021). Miss Jackson vows to keep in touch with the staff and her representative to ensure that the voices of students in her small-group class and others like them are heard at the federal level.

In Conclusion

At Lakeside High, the work prompted by Miss Jackson, including the creation of an equity team, use of disaggregated data, and professional developments, resulted in open and honest communication among stakeholders. Overall, teachers appreciate getting the opportunity to learn strategies to better support their students. Many mentioned that they had never considered that implementing culturally responsive practices could be so simple. Teachers commit to recognizing their implicit biases and implementing more culturally responsive practices. Miss Jackson's advocacy work also pays off within other spheres of influence. For example, she can spend more instructional time supporting the needs of her students, her students feel better understood and respected, students across the state have better prepared teachers, and federal policy makers understand the benefits of culturally responsive practices.

As you set out to advocate for remedying inequities affecting students with disabilities and their families and teachers, it is essential to remain patient and persistent. Advocacy is not always as simple as our vignettes may make it appear. It is easy to be discouraged by a lack of immediate progress, especially for issues regarding equity. However, widespread and systemic change often happens over time, and much of the practice of advocacy centers on providing evidence for why an issue is important and needs remedying. This process can involve much research and persuasion, which can take a significant amount of time. Depending on your ask and the ring from which you are advocating, some changes can occur faster than others. If you follow the steps in this book, extend your advocacy to the five rings of influence, and remain persistent, you will prompt change, and your students and community will be better for it.

WHERE CAN I FIND MORE INFORMATION ABOUT INEQUITIES IN SPECIAL EDUCATION?

Significant Disproportionality in Special Education by State

 On this website administered by the US Department of Education you can explore, by state and territory, levels of significant disproportionality. Visit https://www2.ed.gov/policy/speced/guid/idea/monitor/sig-dispro-reports-part-b .html#resources.

School Discipline for Students with Disabilities

 Understood.com clearly explains legal protections afforded to students with disabilities. They also discuss topics such as changes in placement, manifestation determination, and serious, more significant disciplinary infractions. Visit https://www.understood.org/en/articles/school-discipline-the-rights-of-students-with-ieps-and-504-plans.

What Is Culturally Responsive Teaching?

 Authors at *Education Weekly* describe the basics of culturally responsive teaching, including relevant terminology, its history and importance, and how you can implement culturally responsive practices in your own classroom. Read it for yourself at https://www.edweek.org/teaching-learning/culturally-responsive-teaching -culturally-responsive-pedagogy/2022/04.

Center for Learner Equity

 The Center for Learner Equity is an advocacy organization that provides research-based guidance to policy makers, education leaders, and advocates to bridge the gap between theory and practice. Visit https://www.centerforlearnerequity.org/.

US Department of Education Office for Civil Rights Guidance on Discipline for Students with Disabilities

 The Office for Civil Rights provided this fact sheet that highlights student discipline procedural safeguards under Section 504 of the Rehabilitation Act of 1973. Learn more at https://www 2.ed.gov/about/offices/list/ocr/docs/504-discipline-factsheet.pdf.

KEY TERMS

cultural competence: The ability to understand, appreciate, and interact with individuals from other cultures.

culturally responsive teaching: A pedagogy that incorporates students' customs, perspectives, characteristics, and lived experiences to improve instruction and encourage students of color to see themselves as valued in academic spaces.

disproportionality: The overrepresentation or underrepresentation of groups of students in comparison to their share of the general population.

equity team: A group of individuals representing various educational stakeholders at a school.

identity politics: Political theory and activism geared at representing specific groups of people based on facets of their identity, such as race, ethnicity, religion, sexual orientation, and other characteristics.

implicit bias: Attitudes or stereotypes we assign to people without conscious knowledge.

inequality: Uneven allocation of resources between two or more people or groups of people.

inequity: Lack of access to opportunities due to historical and/or contextual factors.

intersectionality: Overlapping facets of our identities (e.g., race, ethnicity, gender, sexual orientation, disability status) that intersect to create unique and dynamic effects and experiences.

learning loss: Loss of knowledge and skills or reversals in academic progress.

privilege: Inherent advantage that a person or group of persons enjoy based on specific characteristics (e.g., race, ethnicity, economic status, religion).

restraint: Restricting students' ability to move their torso, arms, legs, or head freely.

seclusion: Confining students alone in a room or area they are not permitted to leave.

socioeconomic status: An economic and sociological measure of a person's work experience and individual or family economic access to resources and social position in relation to others.

DISCUSSION QUESTIONS

1. What issues of educational inequities have you experienced or are aware of?
2. What do you think of Miss Jackson's advocacy efforts?
3. How can you get more involved in state and/or federal advocacy efforts for issues that you care about?
4. Identify obstacles Miss Jackson might encounter as she advocates across the five rings.
5. How would you use the five rings of advocacy to advocate in a similar situation?

REFERENCES

Anastasiou, D., Morgan, P. L., Farkas, G., & Wiley, A. L. (2017). Minority disproportionate representation in special education: Politics and evidence, issues, and implications. In *Handbook of special education* (pp. 897–910). Routledge.

Anderson, J. A., Howland, A. A., & McCoach, D. B. (2015). Parental characteristics and resiliency in identification rates for special education. *Preventing School Failure: Alternative Education for Children and Youth, 59*(2), 63–72. https://doi.org/1 0.1080/1045988X.2013.83781

Anspach R. R. (1979). From stigma to identity politics: Political activism among the physically disabled and former mental patients. *Social Science & Medicine, 13,* 765–773.

Bal, A., Sullivan, A. L., & Harper, J. (2014). A situated analysis for special education disproportionality for systemic transformation in an urban school district. *Remedial and Special Education, 35*(1), 3–14. https://doi.org/10.1177/0741932513507754

Barrett, N., McEachin, A., Mills, J. N., & Valant, J. (2017). What are the sources of school discipline disparities by student race and family income? *Education Research Alliance for New Orleans.*

Bernstein, M. (2005). Identity politics. *Annual Review of Sociology, 31*, 47–74. http://www.jstor.org/stable/29737711

Crenshaw, K. (2018). Demarginalizing the intersection of race and sex: A Black feminist critique of antidiscrimination doctrine, feminist theory, and antiracist politics. In K. T. Bartlett & R. Kennedy (Eds.), *Feminist legal theory* (pp. 57–80). Routledge.

Education Recovery Scorecard. (2022, October 28). *New research provides the first clear picture of learning loss at local level.* [Press Release]. https://educationre-coveryscorecard.org/2022/10/28/new-research-provides-the-first-clear-picture-of-learning-loss-at-local-level/

Gage, N. A., Pico, D. L., & Evanovich, L. (2020). National trends and school-level predictors of restraint and seclusion for students with disabilities. *Exceptionality, 30*(1), 1–13. https://doi.org/10.1080/09362835.2020.1727327

Gordon, N. (2018, January 19). Disproportionality in student discipline: Connecting policy to research. *Education Next.* https://www.educationnext.org/disproportionality-student-discipline-connecting-policy-research/

Green, A. L., Cohen, D. R., & Stormont, M. (2019). Addressing and preventing disproportionality in exclusionary discipline practices for students of color with disabilities. *Intervention in School and Clinic, 54*(4), 241–245. https://doi.org/10.1177/1053451218782437

Individuals with Disabilities Education Act of 2004, 20 U.S.C. § 1400.

Kauffman, J. M., Nelson, C. M., Simpson, R. L., & Mock Ward, D. (2017). Contemporary issues. In J. M. Kauffman, D. P. Hallahan, & P. C. Pullen (Eds.), *Handbook of special education* (2nd ed.). Routledge. https://doi.org/10.4324/9781315517698

Keeping All Students Safe Act, H.R. 3474, 117 Cong. (2021). https://www.congress.gov/bill/117th-congress/house-bill/3474/text

McIntosh K., Barnes A., Eliason B., & Morris K. (2014). *Using discipline data within SWPBIS to identify and address disproportionality: A guide for school teams.* Center on PBIS. https://www.pbis.org/resource/using-discipline-data-within-swpbis-to-identify-and-address-disproportionality-a-guide-for-school-teams

Morgan, P. L., Farkas, G., Hillemeier, M. M., & Maczuga, S. (2017). Replicated evidence of racial and ethnic disparities in disability identification in U.S. schools. *Educational Researcher, 46*(6), 305–322. https://doi.org/10.3102/0013189X17726282

National Association of Secondary School Principals. (2020). *Building equity by studying data and understanding the need for change.* https://www.nassp.org/publication/principal-leadership/volume-20/principal-leadership-march-2020/addressing-disproportionate-discipline/

National Center for Learning Disabilities. (2017). *Significant disproportionality in special education: Current trends and actions for impact.* https://www.ncld.org/wp-content/uploads/2020/10/2020-NCLD-Disproportionality_Trends-and-Actions-for-Impact_FINAL-1.pdf

Skiba, R. J., Horner, R. H., Chung, C.-G., Rausch, M. K., May, S. L., & Tobin, T. (2011). Race is not neutral: A national investigation of African American and Latino disproportionality in school discipline. *School Psychology Review, 40*(1), 85–107. https://doi.org/10.1080/02796015.2011.12087730

Stelitano, L., Ekin, S., & Morando Rhim, L. (2022). *How has the pandemic affected students with disabilities? An update on the evidence: Fall 2022.* Center on Reinventing Public Education. https://crpe.org/wp-content/uploads/Special-Education-Impact-Brief_v3.pdf

Sullivan, A. L., Van Norman, E. R., & Klingbeil, D. A. (2014). Exclusionary discipline of students with disabilities: Student and school characteristics predicting suspension. *Remedial and Special Education, 35*(4), 199–210. https://doi.org/10.1177/0741932513519825

Tarrow, S. (1998). *Power in movement.* Cambridge University Press.

US Department of Education. (2012). *Restraint and seclusion: Resource document.* https://www2.ed.gov/policy/seclusion/restraints-and-seclusion-resources.pdf

US Department of Education. (2016). *Dear colleague letter: Restraint and seclusion of students with disabilities.* https://www2.ed.gov/about/offices/list/ocr/letters/colleague-201612-504-restraint-seclusion-ps.pdf

US Department of Education. (2021). *43rd annual report to Congress on the implementation of the Individuals with Disabilities Education Act, 2021.* https://sites.ed.gov/idea/files/43rd-arc-for-idea.pdf

US Department of Education. (2022). *Significant disproportionality reporting under IDEA part B.* https://www2.ed.gov/policy/speced/guid/idea/monitor/sig-dispro reports-part-b.html

Zhang, D., Katsiyannis, A., & Herbst, M. (2004). Disciplinary exclusions in special education: A 4-year analysis. *Behavioral Disorders, 29*(4), 337–347. https://doi.org/10.1177/019874290402900402

Zhang, D., Katsiyannis, A., Ju, S., & Roberts, E. (2014). Minority representation in special education: 5-year trends. *Journal of Child and Family Studies, 23*(1), 118–127. https://doi.org/10.1007/s10826-012-9698-6

Index

About the Authors

Andrew M. Markelz is an associate professor in the Department of Special Education, assistant department chair, and director of Graduate Studies at Ball State University. Dr. Markelz is editor of the *Journal of Special Education Preparation* and co-author of *The Essentials of Special Education Law*. Dr. Markelz is committed to expediting the novice-to-expert teaching curve by preparing special educators to implement proactive classroom management strategies and develop meaningful and legally defensible individualized education programs according to special education law.

Sarah A. Nagro is an associate professor in the Division of Special Education and Disability Research, director of the Interdisciplinary Center for Research and Development in Teacher Education, and professor in charge of the Special Education PhD specialization at George Mason University. Dr. Nagro is committed to identifying best practices for preparing profession-ready teachers who can sustain and grow in the profession to improve the learning experiences of all students including students with disabilities.

Kevin Monnin is a doctoral fellow in the Special Education Program at George Mason University. His research interests focus on studying strategies to attract, prepare, and retain high-quality teachers, often including nontraditional methods for preparing teachers in high-needs fields. Mr. Monnin previously worked as a special education teacher for Fairfax County Public Schools in Virginia. He earned his Master of Education in special education at George Mason University and received his bachelor's in Government and International Politics.

David F. Bateman is a principal researcher at the American Institutes for Research. He is a former due process hearing officer for Pennsylvania for hundreds of hearings. He uses his knowledge of litigation relating to special education to assist school districts in providing appropriate supports for students with disabilities and to prevent and to recover from due process hearings. He has been a classroom teacher of students with learning disabilities, behavior disorders, intellectual disability, and hearing impairments. Dr. Bateman earned a PhD in special education from the University of Kansas and has published numerous articles and books pertaining to special education law and administration.